"I am encouraged by the bold steps taken by Drs. Swaminathan and Mulvihill in challenging members of the research community to embrace a critical approach. Given the seriousness of the times, their work succinctly confronts the dangerous return to research paradigms rooted in theories of deficit, marginalization, and White supremacy. For these reasons, I am indebted to their contribution."

David Stovall, *Professor of Educational Policy Studies and African-American Studies, University of Illinois at Chicago*

"Swaminathan and Mulvihill tend to the important process of formulating questions throughout the entire qualitative research process; it is not relegated to the beginning of the process. Theirs is a critical process of questioning that engages scholars at every aspect of the research process and, as such, provides the opportunity for a deeper, richer inquiry. This book is important for critical scholars who find it imperative to go beyond traditional ways of knowing and doing qualitative research."

Penny A. Pasque, *Brian E. & Sandra O'Brien Presidential Professor, University of Oklahoma*

CRITICAL APPROACHES TO QUESTIONS IN QUALITATIVE RESEARCH

Learning how to formulate questions that examine the power relations between the researcher and participants is at the heart of critical approaches. This book provides a comprehensive overview and treatment of critical approaches to questions in qualitative research. It also examines questions as tools for strategic thinking and decision making at all stages of the qualitative research process. Written using examples from research and teaching, it situates constructing and formulating questions as a critical aspect of qualitative research that encourages learning to interrogate, and inquire, against the grain.

The authors illustrate the ways in which different research questions necessitate different methodological choices, framing questions for research, interviewing, and analysis—suggesting some questions that can guide the writing process. With exercises, sample questions, and outlines for planning research, this book assists qualitative researchers with creating more effective questions, including formulating questions to guide reflexivity meant to confront prevailing assumptions and therefore dismantle and uncover omissions and invisibilities.

This book stands out among other qualitative research methods books in its focus on critical approaches to questions as the driver of the research imagination. Utilizing a number of examples, there is also a focused discussion of how to arrive at research questions, align interview questions with those research questions, actively construct questions to guide the data analysis process, and use further types of questions to guide the writing process. The examples the authors employ include questions drawn from qualitative approaches to phenomenology, ethnography, life writing, feminist research, and participatory action research.

Raji Swaminathan, Ph.D., is an Associate Professor in the Department of Educational Policy and Community Studies at the University of Wisconsin-Milwaukee. Her research and teaching interests are in the areas of emerging methods in qualitative research, urban education, and alternative education.

Thalia M. Mulvihill, Ph.D., Professor of Social Foundations and Higher Education at Ball State University, serves as President of the International Society for Educational Biography and the Secretary for the AERA Biographical and Documentary Research SIG. Her areas of expertise include qualitative research methods, life writing, innovative pedagogies, history, and sociology of higher education.

CRITICAL APPROACHES TO QUESTIONS IN QUALITATIVE RESEARCH

Raji Swaminathan and
Thalia M. Mulvihill

NEW YORK AND LONDON

First published 2017
by Routledge
711 Third Avenue, New York, NY 10017

and by Routledge
2 Park Square, Milton Park, Abingdon, Oxon OX14 4RN

Routledge is an imprint of the Taylor & Francis Group, an informa business

British Library Cataloguing-in-Publication Data
A catalogue record for this book is available from the British Library

Library of Congress Cataloging-in-Publication Data
A catalog record for this book has been requested

ISBN: 978-1-138-64298-0 (hbk)
ISBN: 978-1-138-64297-3 (pbk)
ISBN: 978-1-315-62960-5 (ebk)

Typeset in Bembo
by Apex CoVantage, LLC

Printed in the United Kingdom
by Henry Ling Limited

CONTENTS

1

BACKGROUND

Questions and the Critical Framework in Qualitative Research

Questions: The Heart of Research

Asking good questions is fundamental to the heart of research, critical thinking, creative thinking, and problem solving. In our deliberations regarding this book, one of the reasons we focused on questions was rooted in our own experiences of research, where our mutual dialogues often took the form of questioning each other and the content of our enterprise. It was in many ways at the heart of the research activity, a space where curiosity was ignited and an excitement to investigate or find out took over.

The rationale for developing a book on this topic is to elevate the much-needed discussion about the nature of the thinking processes needed in order to design critical approaches that are innovative and successful. Our aim is to provide a comprehensive overview of critical approaches to questions in qualitative research. To us, questions represent a key competency in conducting research. We use "questions" as a way to work against prescriptive and mechanical how-tos and instead discuss them as an overarching strategy to stimulate qualitative thinking for research purposes. Qualitative thinking has been defined by several scholars (Saldana, 2015; Vagle, 2014) as eschewing a single point of view or the seeking of an "objective truth" in favor of drawing on multiple perspectives and diverse ways of thinking; observing events, scenes, and people; discussing, interviewing, and analyzing talk and text; and constructing stories from listening deeply to participants' views of phenomena. Such thinking draws on art and creativity, as well as planned, systematic categorization leading to new insights about phenomena under inquiry. We utilize "questions" to stimulate wonder, curiosity, and mystery during the lifecycle of the research process.

Despite our acknowledgement that questions are at the center of research, our aim in this book is to resist thinking about questions as a necessity but instead conceptualize questions as a tool that can stimulate different types of thinking. The objective of this book is to provide a synthesis of how scholars have approached the subject of questions in qualitative research along with practical suggestions on how to use questions as a stimulus to thinking throughout the process of research. How do questions serve as tools for the planning and implementation of a study, for analysis of data, and for writing up research? To this end, we discuss how questions have been raised in the literature, but we also provide the qualitative researcher who wishes to undertake a project with tools that can be adapted to specific projects. The questions and suggestions for question generation that are presented in this book are not prescriptive but emerge from our own experiences of research and teaching. It is our intent, through examining and centralizing questions in qualitative research, to keep alive the mystery and wonder of research.

Whom Is this Book for?

We aim to provide a comprehensive discussion of questions through the lifecycle of the research process. The critical paradigm is central to this endeavor; however the book can be used by any qualitative researcher who wants to get an overview of the effective use of questions in qualitative research. We direct this book toward students of qualitative research and academic scholars who may want to use it as a companion book in their courses. Scholars affiliated with the social sciences, health sciences, and humanities can all use this book. In addition, those who are writing their theses or dissertations and are seeking to use different approaches will also find this book useful.

What Is the Book About?

In this book, we present questions as tools for strategic thinking and decision-making in the research process. Maxwell (2005) suggests that questions are at the "hub" or "heart" of research and emerge from the design while other researchers (Metz, 2001) suggest that questions are the starting point of research. Although they may differ on when questions should be posed, scholars are in agreement that questions undergird the research process and the strength of the research project is often dependent on the quality of questions posed by researchers. Yet, as we have frequently found in our classes, students often cannot initially distinguish between research questions (RQs) and interview questions (IQs). And further, students have difficulty understanding the variety of ways that interviews can be designed (e.g., structured, semi-structured, unstructured) and how to make these types of design decisions. Most existing textbooks on qualitative research methods embed the sections dealing with questions in relevant chapters (see for example, Bogdan and Biklen, 2003; Creswell, 2013; Flick, 2009; Hatch, 2002; Maxwell, 2012) and tend to focus most attention on research questions and interview questions. However, they do not devote much space to ways to formulate questions during the data-analysis process, or during the various stages of reflexivity, or the time when you pull the whole manuscript together working and reworking during the revisions process. Further interrogating the range of ways questions can be used as dynamic tools, and recognizing that we, as qualitative researchers, can elevate our abilities to formulate and use these tools, is the driving motivation for our explorations within this book.

We provide a focused discussion of questions in qualitative research through the full lifecycle of the research process. While some articles in the qualitative literature discuss question generation, they are few (see McCaslin and Scott [2003] and White [2013] for a more recent example). There is a need to bring together, in one place, critical approaches to questions in qualitative research.

Qualitative research methodologists (Burns and Grove, 1999; Creswell, 2013; Morse, 1994) distinguish between different approaches to qualitative research and point out the types of questions asked in each research approach. They emphasize that the type of question asked depends on the paradigm or epistemology underlying each type of approach. For example, Morse (1994) explains that questions for a phenomenological study would differ from that of an ethnography or a grounded study. The field of qualitative research is quite expansive, including qualitative studies that are participatory action research or feminist research; yet anywhere on the spectrum of qualitative inquiry, questions are a central feature. Our aim with this book is to focus on critical approaches to questions in qualitative research while recognizing the larger surrounding critical framework we have chosen to explore. In this chapter we provide an overview of the ways in which scholars and researchers within the critical paradigm have approached discussions regarding questions and the importance of questions in qualitative research. We examine and describe assumptions of the critical paradigm that guide the framing of questions.

What Do We Mean By Critical Approaches?

Kuntz (2015) points out that the term "critical" has been overused to the point of not meaning anything anymore. A book titled *Critical Approaches*, therefore, needs to be explained. For us, the use of the term "critical" in "critical approaches" is to indicate an interest not only with procedures, but more importantly, the rationale behind such approaches, as well as to draw attention to the process in research that goes backstage and asks, "Why do researchers make the choices they do?" If questions are the mainstay of research, what would critical approaches to questions in the research process look like? To do this, we draw on the literature and give examples from researchers' studies and their methodological notes to point out the ways in which they made decisions and how these examples can guide the researcher to an understanding of the rationale for such decision-making. Kuntz (2015) uses the term "critical" to mean intervention, drawn from the work of Kincheloe and McLaren (2005), and it has a social justice goal. Our use of the term "approaches" clarifies our intent not to prescribe a single model or method. Critical approaches to questions is as much a tool for critique as it is a way to release the imagination. It requires a look beyond the immediate, to question that which we take for granted and seek connections between seemingly disparate ideas; it is an approach that nurtures creativity. This is in line with Harvey's (2001) idea of critical geography, in which he explains that critical scholarship exposes the "artificiality of the separation between fact and value" (p. 36). By critical approaches to questions, we hope to resist the practice of positioning the methodologist as a technocrat (Kuntz, 2015) and to invoke a vocabulary that embraces the messiness of the research process.

Critical approaches can be situated among the spectrum of approaches that currently exist. Our view of "critical" is focusing on the paradigm broadly, not narrowly on "critical qualitative research projects," as this is in fact antithetical to the "critical" paradigm and not as an either/or juxtaposition to other related paradigms, such as the interpretive paradigm. Rather "critical approaches" are meant to make everpresent the power issues inherent in all research endeavors, with an eye toward social change. We are advocating for a nesting relationship between "designing questions for qualitative research projects" and using critical approaches when designing questions for qualitative research projects. It is more than semantics and it is important to clarify our terms and meanings and to be cognizant of the various starting points different reading audiences might occupy as they enter this book.

Our use of the term "critical" connotes the nurturing of an attitude and sensibility that encompasses the following:

1. The capacity to interrogate and inquire against the grain;
2. The skill to ask questions that confront prevailing assumptions leading to an analysis, dismantling and uncovering of omissions and invisibilities;
3. Paying increased attention to power and privilege;
4. Learning to eschew "absolute truth" in favor of multiple or "partial" truths and perspectives;
5. Privileging the perspectives of the marginalized for purposes of empowerment, equity, and freedom;
6. Examining context and structure along with individual agency;
7. Using questions to challenge neoliberal ways of knowing and the conditions giving rise to them; and
8. Resisting atomization of the research process and the researcher.

The above components comprise an attitude that takes into account a humanistic and critical framework—at once paying attention to issues of power and rights within an ethic of care.

Critical Approaches and the Role of the Researcher

Critical approaches to questions means approaching questions from a variety of perspectives to uncover assumptions, analyze issues of power that are visible and invisible, and examine omissions. We want researchers to engage in a discussion on multiple truths rather than remain neutral or passive in the face of taken-for-granted assumptions about research. The intent is to stimulate the questioning of statements such as "the data revealed" that indicate data speaking for themselves that obscures the role and the responsibility of the methodologist. There is a need for a balance between alignment of methodology with research questions and interview questions and the necessarily messy nature of qualitative research that eludes and resists the grasp of neat categories or consistent themes. We situate this book broadly within the critical paradigm since contemporary qualitative researchers use the critical paradigm extensively. Newer strands of qualitative research such as indigenous research, cultural research, feminist research, and narrative research are all situated within the critical paradigm. In order to better understand the term "critical," our own experiences of being regarded as the "methodologist" on dissertation committees inform this discussion. As Kuntz (2015) mentions in narrating his experiences, we too are often persuaded to be on dissertation committees as the "expert qualitative methodologist," a position that reduces the dissertation process into a series of parts and loses sight of the interwoven character of the intellectual enterprise in research. It sets apart method as a technique rather than as a thoughtful process—a process that cannot be separated from the rest of the research undertaking: the content, the questions asked, the analysis, and the review of literature.

Kuntz (2015) argues that neoliberal discourses have allowed the methodologist to assume the role of a technocrat and suggests that methodologists need to refuse to allow themselves to be boxed into such roles. We consider "critical approaches" in qualitative research to work against compartmentalization and instead regard the whole research endeavor as a meaningful and imaginative act. Research from a critical perspective would work to counter neoliberal conditions where "power [is] applied . . . through the normalizing use of statistics" (Newheiser, 2016, p. 3) or where market forces enter noneconomic areas of life (Sandel, 2013), resulting in people being known as parts of a whole, or in the language of Deleuze (1995) as "dividuals," by which process people are turned into data bits. An example of such a process would be to identify a person's health in terms of blood pressure counts or their cholesterol count and a person's economic wealth by credit scores. Crawford, Miltner and Gray (2014) argue that data and statistics and the advent of big data routinely separate the powerless from the powerful, those who can analyze the data and those who cannot, thus creating new pockets of privilege in society. We argue that in research, a desire for objectivity and neutrality may well crowd out concerns of social justice by stripping context from such data pieces. Research driven by data bits at the expense of the human experience would result in a loss of social responsibility (Giroux, 2014). Critical approaches to qualitative research work against such loss and are indisputably tied to social responsibility.

Eco (2015) points out that "social science methodology has fetishized quantitative statistical methods, producing enormous studies that are dense with data but not useful for understanding real phenomena" (Section 2.6.2). The representation of an individual solely through numbers can be dehumanizing. Critical approaches works to correct such partial views in research through examining how people make meaning of their lives and how they represent their lived experiences.

Critical approaches introduce complexity on the one hand while offering tools and strategies on the other. The latter is a way into "deep work" (Newport, 2016) rather than a way out of complex thinking. Tools and strategies to create questions that can serve as catalysts to one's creative and critical thinking or that which can disrupt habitual patterns are needed. Thus critical approaches ask the researcher to be methodologically naive (Bennett, 2010) and allow oneself to be uncertain and engage in what Rebecca Solnit (2005) refers to as "the art of being at home in the unknown [and] being at home with being lost" (p. 22). However, this step away from the position of a researcher as neutral observer does not signal a move towards a relativistic claim on reality—in other words, it does not mean that a researcher's positionality allows only for commentary on "insider" research. It does mean, however, that critical approaches ask that researchers take on challenges that are also ethically grounded and responsible, as well as to be ready to face the uncertainty of not quite knowing what results the research will produce.

Alvesson and Skoldberg (2000) outlined three versions of critical approaches to qualitative research that also meet the emancipatory ideal of the critical paradigm. In the first, they cite the work of Thomas (1993), who outlines some key characteristics of critical qualitative research. These include subject matter or a focus on questions that have to do with injustice or control, an attention to power issues, an emphasis on researcher reflexivity, a skeptical stance towards data, and a focus on reporting ideas that go against prevailing thought. In the second version, they advocate an "intensive critical interpretation or close reading" (p. 141). In the third version, the critical researcher works at the theoretical level using existing studies and adding a small study of her own. In this instance, the study would be regarded as part of the larger work and not subject to the intensive critical approach.

Critical approaches to research require an attention and action that interrupt one's own habitual patterns of thought. As Kuntz (2015) explains, researchers often engage in the "logics of extraction" almost habitually and without enough thought given to the assumptions behind such procedural concerns. He gives the example of interview as a method for gathering data in which a person's sense of being and experience is converted into a disembodied digital voice and then to text and "extracted" into the final report in the form of excerpts of data. His concern for the loss of the whole person in such cases is an echo of the work of feminist scholars. Feminists have long argued that the editing of the voices of participants can sometimes lead us away from those new interpretations or constructs that are required for us to make meaning of experiences not yet articulated or less voiced in the dominant discourse (Devault, 1990). A critical approach to questions is rooted in the reflexivity of the researcher.

Critical Approaches to Questions

Critical approaches to questions in research would mean encouraging researchers to use reflexivity to challenge assumptions and conventional modes of thinking. Reflexivity means being aware of oneself in the process of reflecting, interviewing, or observing. It means learning to examine why we think what we think. It means analyzing hidden assumptions that grow into habitual patterns of thought. It also means deliberately setting out to interrupt such patterns of thinking so that researchers would reframe questions and ask questions that push at the boundaries of their frame of reference. For example, in place of the question "why don't workers work harder?" (Burawoy, 1979), they might ask "why do workers work as hard as they do?" This promotes a different type of thinking that is counter to prevailing expectations. In order for researchers to undertake research that goes against dominant patterns, it may require researchers to be reflective and reflexive, to ponder upon what they are interested in, and also to ask how their own positionality intersects with the questions of their investigation. Since researchers are susceptible to being socialized into dominant thought patterns, questions that stimulate critical and reflexive thinking can be useful tools for strategic interventions.

Critical Thinking as a Basis for Questions

> Critical thinking is a desire to seek, patience to doubt, fondness to meditate, slowness to assert, readiness to consider, carefulness to dispose and set in order; and hatred for every kind of imposture.
> Francis Bacon (1605)

Developing the ability to formulate and pursue different types of qualitative inquiry questions requires a strong conceptual and practical foundation in critical thinking, an ever-expanding researcher's imagination (Mulvihill and Swaminathan, 2012) that engages with the human condition through portals of wonder and curiosity, and a propensity to enjoy the central tenet of mystery whereby certainty is not deemed possible. Hansen (2012) reminds us that qualitative researchers are involved in an "existential awakening and [a process of] coming-to-the-world-as-if-for-the-first-time" (Hansen, 2012, p. 3). Hansen (2012) further reminds us that Socratic questioning is "led and nurtured by a fundamental lived experience of wonder (*Thaumazein*), which is not to be confused with a conceptual and epistemological puzzlement and deadlock (*Aporia*)" (Hansen, 2012, p. 3). And he cautions that if the

> use of methods and techniques is not governed by a higher musicality for the "subject matter" (the living phenomenon) then the phenomenological researcher will become just an "epistemological bookkeeper"; one who may be an expert in systemizing and analyzing data but who does not have the necessary phenomenological "ear" to hear the phenomenon itself (*die Sache selbst*).
> (Hansen, 2012, p. 4)

While Hansen is building arguments specifically for phenomenologists, his basic premises are applicable for all qualitative researchers.

Socratic Questioning and Critical Thinking

Socratic questioning and other critical thinking tools offer qualitative researchers exciting opportunities to diversify their understanding and use of questions. While there is an extensive literature on the uses of Socratic Questioning for pedagogical purposes, it is rarely applied to the thinking used to develop and carry out qualitative inquiry projects. For example, Paul and Elder (2007) offer six types of Socratic questions (see below), which can be used not only to illustrate the complex variety of questions available to us as qualitative researchers but also the various categories under which we can develop specific questions. Consider how these categories could be used to prompt the development of questions at different stages of a research project:

1. Questioning clarity: questions that assist with elaboration, illustration, exemplifiers
2. Questioning precision: questions that seek more details, more specifics
3. Questioning accuracy: questions that assist with evaluating trustworthiness of claims
4. Questioning relevance: questions that help ascertain reasonable connections and appropriate focus

5.   Questioning depth: questions that explore levels of simplicity and levels of complexity

6.   Questioning breadth: questions that examine from multiple points of view or frames of reference (paraphrased from Paul and Elder, 2007, p. 32).

Here are some examples of how these categories can be used to help aid our thinking about designing useful questions for qualitative inquiry projects.

Try It Out: Research Journal Exercise 1.1

Using Table 1.1 sketch out several questions for each stage of your qualitative research project using all six categories of questions for each stage.

In addition to Socratic questioning, there are other useful typologies of questions that can further assist qualitative researchers. One such typology can look at questions as a broad sweep across the process of research. These typologies are to serve as catalysts for your thinking about your research project and to allow the time to immerse yourself in the topic.

TABLE 1.1 Six Categories of Questions Per Each Stage of Qualitative Research Project

Research Project Stages	Clarity	Precision	Accuracy	Relevance	Depth	Breadth
Purpose Statement and RQs						
Literature Review						
Data Collection (e.g., Interview Questions)						
Data Analysis						
Discussion and Implications of Findings						
Further Research						

A Typology of Thematic Questions

Qualitative researchers can clarify their research projects by working through and thinking about each of the following:

The Concept or the Idea Question: This represents what concept the researcher might want to investigate further. For example, we might want to know: How do different people define friendship? What is bullying? How do teenagers define bullying?

The Learning Question: Once a concept is identified, we might want to ask: Where would I learn about this? In the above example, we would want to find out and identify how best to learn about friendship or bullying.

The Context Question: The context that frames the study needs to be identified. Do we want to learn about friendship in the context of teenagers, activities pursued by youth, or friendship among neighbors?

The Historical Question: How has this concept or idea changed over time? How was it practiced in the past? For example, cyber bullying did not occur before internet use. The use of the internet brought with it a different type of friendship and bullying. Friends do not need to stay in geographical proximity to be regarded as friends and friendship itself can be defined in a variety of ways since the advent of Facebook.

The Setting Question: What is the setting in which we want to study the phenomenon or activity? Is there something we can learn from the place or setting? Why is this my choice of setting?

The Participant Question: Why am I choosing this particular set of people or places or activities? How can they advance my understanding of my research question?

The Values Question: How do my values play a role in the research?

The Value Question: Who will find this research valuable and why?

Use the above questions and try them out on your own research. Research Journal Exercise 1.2 gives you some suggestions and prompts for your research journal.

Try It Out: Research Journal Exercise 1.2

In your research journal write about the following:

1) What is the topic you are interested in?
2) How can you learn more about this topic?
3) Where can you find this phenomenon occurring?
4) What is the history of this topic? How has it changed over time?
5) Why engage this particular group of people in your study? What ties them together? Whom would you not consider to be part of your study and why? What are reasonable alternatives?
6) How does your background and identity (cultural, family, class, race, gender) predispose you towards viewing the phenomenon you are investigating and the participants? Does it predispose you to view them favorably or negatively?
7) What situations either make you comfortable or uncomfortable? Do you think you might encounter such situations? How will you deal with such circumstances?

How Have Scholars Discussed Questions?

Questions have been discussed in connection with the purpose of the study or while formulating the problem for which research needs to be carried out. The purpose of qualitative research often takes the form of describing, exploring, and explaining phenomena being studied. Qualitative research questions often take the form of *what is this?* or *what is happening here?* and are more concerned with the process rather than the outcome. While questions are undoubtedly central to qualitative research, textbooks on qualitative research neverthe-less tend to confine discussions on questions to sections on research design or data collection (see for example, Bogdan and Biklen, 2003; Creswell, 2013; Flick, 2009; Hatch, 2002; Maxwell, 2012). Other references to questions are usually placed throughout the text. What is missing is a comprehensive and focused discussion of questions in qualitative research and the tools to be able to formulate clear ques-tions and to use questions as strategic devices.

Research questions cannot be confined to the beginning of the research process and are always evolving (Creswell, 2013). Schol-ars agree that questions can change during the process of research (Charmaz, 2006; Creswell, 2013) and that new questions are asked at different stages of research. The process of generating questions is critical to qualitative work during the research design, data collec-tion, analysis, and writing processes, as well as for theoretical consid-erations. All these demand an ongoing reflexivity on the part of the researcher, a state of mind that seeks to "maintain the state of doubt and to carry on systematic and protracted inquiry" (John Dewey, 1910/1971, p. 3). Researchers (Burns and Grove, 1999; Creswell, 2013; Morse, 1994) distinguish between different approaches to qualitative research and point out the differences between research approaches and the types of questions asked in each research approach. They emphasize that the type of question asked depends on the paradigm or epistemology underlying each type of approach. For example, Morse (1994) explains that questions for a phenomeno-logical study would differ from that of an ethnography or a grounded study. The distinctions between these approaches are elaborated in the second chapter of this book.

What Is Missing in Researching the "Gap"

Several scholars have pointed out that questions for research emerge from "gaps" in the existing literature. In formulating research ques-tions in qualitative research, several issues and factors come into play. We read the literature, identify what is missing or mis-stated or even under-emphasized, and then formulate a question that links these "gaps" to our research interest. While this aspect of coming to research questions has been described in texts on methodology in a fairly procedural manner, it leaves out important factors such as the curiosity of the researcher, the unique way of thinking about and analyzing the problem that a researcher might have, and the intuitive thinking that accompanies the process. The biography of the researcher is missing in the descriptions of objectively examining the "gaps" in literature. We do not mean to suggest that researching gaps is not crucial; instead, we draw your attention to the factors that are usually obscured that provide the link between the researcher's interest and the particular gap in the literature.

In qualitative research, questions represent possibilities and are integral to the process of understanding the worlds of participants' lives and perspectives. They provide the occasion for the co-construction of knowledge. They offer the telling of stories rather than producing answers.

Our intent is to stimulate the questioning of statements such as "the data revealed" or "the data show" that indicate data speaking for themselves and obscures the role and the responsibility of the methodologist.

In this chapter, we have outlined what we mean by critical approaches to questions and laid the foundation for the chapters to follow. In the following chapters, we elaborate on procedures for arriving at different types of questions during the qualitative research process as well as ways to critically approach such a process.

Any questions so far? :)

References

Alvesson, M., & Skoldberg, K. (2000). *Reflexive methodology: New vistas for qualitative research.* Thousand Oaks, CA: Sage.

Bennett, J. (2010). *Vibrant matter: A political ecology of things.* Durham, NC: Duke University Press.

Bogdan, R., & Biklen, S. (2003). *Qualitative research for education: An introduction to theories and methods.* Boston, MA: Allyn & Bacon.

Burawoy, M. (1979). *Manufacturing consent.* Chicago, IL: Chicago University Press.

Burns, N., & Grove, S.K. (1999). *Understanding nursing research.* Philadelphia, PA: W.B. Saunders Company.

Charmaz, K. (2006). *Constructing grounded theory: A practical guide through qualitative research*. London: Sage.

Crawford, K., Miltner, K., & Gray, M.L. (2014). Big data | critiquing big data: Politics, ethics, epistemology. Special section introduction. *International Journal of Communication, 8*, 1663–1672.

Creswell, J.W. (2013). *Qualitative inquiry and research design choosing among five approaches*. Thousand Oaks, CA: Sage.

Deleuze, G. (1995). *Difference and repetition*. New York, NY: Columbia University Press.

Devault, M.L. (1990). Talking and listening from women's standpoint: Feminist strategies for interviewing and analysis. *Social Problems, 37*(1), 96–116. Retrieved from http://doi.org.proxy.bsu.edu/10.2307/800797

Dewey, J. (1910/1971). *How we think*. New York, NY: Prometheus Books.

Eco, U. (2015). *How to write a thesis*. Boston, MA: MIT Press.

Flick, U. (2009). *An introduction to qualitative research*. London: Sage.

Giroux, H. (2014). Public intellectuals against the neoliberal university. In N. Denzin & M. Giardina (Eds.), *Qualitative inquiry outside the academy* (pp. 35–60). Walnut Creek, CA: Left Coast Press.

Hansen, F.T. (2012). One step further: The dance between poetic dwelling and Socratic wonder in phenomenological research. *Indo-Pacific Journal of Phenomenology, 12*(2), 1–20.

Harvey, D. (2001). *Spaces of capital: Towards a critical geography*. New York, NY: Routledge.

Hatch, J.A. (2002, August 1). *Doing qualitative research in education settings*. Albany: SUNY Press.

Kincheloe, J., & Mclaren, P. (2005). Rethinking critical theory and qualitative research. In Norman K. Denzin & Yvonna S. Lincoln (Eds.), *The Sage handbook of qualitative research* (3rd ed., pp. 303–342). London: Sage.

Kuntz, A. (2015). *The responsible methodologist: Inquiry, truth-telling and social justice*. Walnut Creek, CA: Left Coast Press.

Maxwell, J.A. (2005). *Qualitative research design* (Vol. 41). Applied social research methods series. Thousand Oaks, CA: Sage.

Maxwell, J.A. (2012). *A realist approach for qualitative research*. Thousand Oaks, CA: Sage.

McCaslin, M.L., & Scott, K.W. (2003). The five-question method for framing a qualitative research study. *The Qualitative Report, 8*(3), 447–461. Retrieved from http://nsuworks.nova.edu/tqr/vol8/iss3/6

Metz, M.H. (2001). Intellectual border crossing in graduate education: A report from the field. *Educational Researcher, 30*(5), 1–7.

Morse, J.M. (1994). *Critical issues in qualitative research methods*. Thousand Oaks, CA: Sage.

Mulvihill, T., & Swaminathan, R. (2012). Nurturing the imagination: Creativity processes and innovative qualitative research projects. *Journal of Educational Psychology*, *5*(4), 1–8.

Newheiser, D. (2016). Foucault, Gary Becker and the critique of neoliberalism. *Theory, Culture and Society*, *33*(5), 3–21.

Newport, C. (2016). *Deep work: Rules for focused success in a distracted world*. Boston, MA: Grand Central Publishing.

Paul, R., & Elder, L. (2007). Critical thinking: The art of Socratic questioning. *Journal of Developmental Education*, *31*(1), 36.

Saldana, J. (2015). *Thinking qualitatively: Methods of mind*. Thousand Oaks, CA: Sage.

Sandel, M. (2013). *What money can't buy*. New York, NY: Farrar, Strauss & Giroux.

Solnit, R. (2005). *A field guide to getting lost*. New York, NY: Viking Press.

Thomas, J. (1993). *Doing critical ethnography*. Newbury Park, CA: Sage.

Vagle, M.D. (2014). *Crafting phenomenological research*. Thousand Oaks, CA: Left Coast Press.

White, P. (2013). Who's afraid of research questions? The neglect of research questions in the methods literature and a call for question-led methods teaching. *International Journal of Research and Method in Education*, *36*(3), 213–227. doi:10.1080/17437 27X.2013.809413.

2

QUESTIONS ALONG THE QUALITATIVE RESEARCH JOURNEY

This chapter explores differences in research questions, data collection questions, analysis questions, and questions for writing. It asks: How do questions differ in varying approaches to qualitative research? It is often difficult to distinguish between questions at different stages of the research; for example, between research questions and questions for data collection or analyses. To facilitate this understanding, this chapter will describe the distinctions via examples of each type of question. In addition, the chapter will discuss the ways to get from a research question to interview questions. This chapter will discuss types of questions for interviews, including reciprocal questioning, dialogue, and discussions and their influences on the power relations between the researcher and participants. Finally, the chapter will discuss questions to facilitate analyses of data within each approach and suggest some questions that can guide the writing of research.

Introduction

How We Know and How We Think: Questions of Epistemology and Theoretical Frameworks

One of the ways in which students approach qualitative research is by first thinking about and articulating a question that is fueled by a compelling curiosity about some phenomenon. It could be: "How do first-generation college students navigate the Ph.D. process?" The question is then quickly linked to a method of collecting data as they consider how they will go about collecting this information: "Perhaps I can interview first-generation college students who received their Ph.D.s in the last ten years?" Arriving at questions in this way may neglect the process of thinking about epistemological assumptions.

Epistemology in simple terms tells us how we know. Common epistemological positions in qualitative research include subjectivism, objectivism, and constructionism (Crotty, 1998):

> Subjectivism: A key concept in qualitative research. It centralizes the knowledge of the experiencer and centralizes the concept that knowledge is generated from the mind. It assumes that we cannot separate ourselves from what we know. The researcher and the subject of research are linked and truth is negotiated.
>
> Objectivism: The researcher is independent of the world and can study the world objectively. This is a key concept in quantitative research. Pure objectivism is critiqued in qualitative approaches.
>
> Constructionism: A key attribute that assumes that knowledge is constructed and derived from larger discourses in society. Language is not neutral and language helps to construct the meaning of reality.

We need to be clear about which epistemological assumptions we are making in our research. Theoretical frameworks are indicators of how we think or how we look or perceive. Frameworks most used in qualitative research are postpositivism, interpretivism, feminism, critical theory, and postmodernism:

> Positivism: The paradigm assumes that we can scientifically find out the rules governing social life. Methodology used for research is usually quantitative.
>
> Interpretivism: The paradigm assumes that knowledge is co-constructed and that the world is interpreted by the actors in it. Methodology used for research is qualitative.
>
> Feminism: The paradigm highlights that the experiences of women in the world are different from men because they occupy

different power positions. Methodology used for research is feminist and qualitative.

Critical theory: The paradigm highlights power and relationships of power with a view to emancipation. It examines the socially and economically disadvantaged groups in society and offers a different stance from which to view society. The research methodology can be a combination of qualitative and quantitative; however, feminist methods, critical race methodology, and methodologies of the oppressed are often used to conduct research in the critical paradigm.

Postmodernism: A stance and paradigm that highlights, critiques, and deconstructs objectivist, imperialist, rationalist, and methodological assumptions of thought and practice. Postmodernism critiques the positivist research paradigm with its assumption of truth and objectivity.

If theoretical frameworks indicate how we think, methodologies represent general strategies of inquiry and a shared understanding of the approach and the justification for using that approach. Methodologies commonly used in qualitative research are feminist, phenomenology, ethnography, and participatory action research. "Method" is the term used to denote detailed plans for gathering data and analyzing the same. Therefore, in a given research project that seeks to understand women's experiences in STEM majors, the framework would be interpretive, methodology would be phenomenology, and the method would likely be interviews. The alignment of research question to the epistemology, methodology, and method is indicative of the quality of a project and often receives favorable reviews. In order to ensure that these aspects of research processes are in alignment, asking the questions outlined below can serve as a reminder.

Alignment of Epistemology, Theoretical Framework, Methodology, and Method

1) What is my worldview or belief system? Do I believe in objectivism (truth is objective and meanings reside in objects outside of human interactions)? Constructionism (I believe that knowledge is constructed through an active engagement with another

and the environment)? Subjectivism (I believe that meanings are imposed by the subjects irrespective of and independent of the object?

2) How does my interest link with my belief system?
3) What prior knowledge do I have about this issue?
4) What is it that I most want to know in this project?
5) What is the best way for me to obtain that information?
6) What is the lens through which I am looking at the situation or phenomenon?
7) If I use a different lens, how will my question change?
8) Is my approach to gathering data appropriate to the type of phenomenon I am investigating?

These questions can serve to align the process of the research with the researcher's belief system and worldview. If a researcher is interested in equity issues, for example, it is unlikely that the researcher would employ a deficit perspective to research how students end up repeating the ninth grade. The researcher would instead be interested in knowing the stories of students who are repeating the ninth grade to understand how that came to take place.

Examples of Further Questions that Stimulate Deep Thinking about the Project

Who is advantaged or disadvantaged from an answer to this question?
What assumptions are taken for granted in this question?

The above questions can facilitate broad-based idea generation or brainstorming within a particular area of interest. Some preliminary questions and methods can also be experimented with and successive drafts of a pictorial representation of these questions and how they relate to each other can aid in developing fledgling ideas into research designs.

Using Questions as Strategy to Find the Study's Focus, Including the Research Questions (RQs)

Qualitative researchers can discover their topic through examining their own autobiography and experiences, through reading about the experiences of others, or through the research interests of their professors. As Flick has observed, research questions often originate with "researchers' personal biographies and their social contexts" (Flick, 2008, p. 109). Thinking back to those moments that have puzzled one or have left questions without easy answers are cues to help discover possible research ideas and topics.

Constructing the Idea/Topic: The Personal Experience and Silence in the Field

The main topic or idea around which a research project is constructed leads from a concern that is stimulated in a variety of ways. Personal experiences can trigger ideas and questions leading to research. Rachel Simmons (2002) looked back to her own experiences of school. Her painful memories of being excluded and losing friendships as a schoolgirl made her wonder if she was the only person who had felt so lonely and miserable in school. The many books on bullying in the library focused on young males and overt physical bullying and failed to resonate with her own experiences of psychologically feeling hurt and left out. The public bullying and fist fights of young males did not come anywhere near explaining the private hostility and aggression that girls expressed towards each other.

Such silences in the literature can indicate a research topic waiting to be taken up and explored. For Simmons, what drove her was her desire to understand what had happened to her and to a large number of women who, like her, had kept these incidents quiet, convinced that they were alone in these experiences. Here was a classic example of a prevalent social problem that she had assumed was a personal issue that pertained only to her. Feminist researchers have often referred to the links between personal and social problems as the "personal is the political."

Qualitative research can also begin with thinking qualitatively about an activity that one experiences. Researchers can be curious about what drives people to participate in activities. Janice Radway in *Reading the Romance* (1984) conducted participant observation in a women's group that read romance novels to find out what they thought of the activity, what women got out of it, and how they discussed the novels they read. Romance reading is usually dismissed as a frivolous and mindless escape; however, Radway found that women reading romance novels, contrary to popular belief, enjoyed women heroines with spunk and spirit, did not like elements of cruelty in male heroes, and "read" and critiqued the romance novels much more deeply than expected. Similarly, women's experiences of sports such as roller derby that go against the conventional ideas of femininity and dislike of contact sports can be researched both by insiders (people who participate in the sport) and by those on the sidelines.

The Research Question: Emerging from Literature or Current Events

Many scholars insist that the best questions are persistent and remain in the mind of the researcher so that they almost always percolate to the top of almost any research endeavor. At times, questions or ideas have long been nurtured in the mind before they are fully articulated or put on paper. Ideas turn into questions, although the source of ideas is often a curiosity to learn something or to puzzle over an issue that is unclear or find a way to right a perceived injustice.

Students engaged in qualitative studies usually learn quickly that the research question is of paramount importance and that without a robust research question, they are unlikely to have a viable study. However, not all qualitative researchers are in agreement regarding when questions should be posed. Some scholars believe that questions emerge from the design (Maxwell, 2005) while others such as Metz (2001) believe that questions are the starting point of research. Still others (for example, those taking the grounded theory approach) prefer to have questions emerge in the field. However, despite such differences, they do agree that the strength of the research project is often dependent on the quality of questions posed by researchers. Mantzoukas (2008) argues that research findings have value only if they provide coherent answers to well-framed questions. A poorly conceived question is unlikely to lead one to a question linked to an issue. Issues can be identified as priorities in the discipline or from current political events. The tragic events of a mass shooting in an

Orlando gay club in Florida in 2016 can lead researchers to ask critical questions regarding identity, voice, marginalization, prejudice, and violence.

Some scholars have suggested that careful selection of a topic is important and ought to be informed by a close reading of the existing literature in order to construct a compelling set of research questions. Students often wonder where to "find" good questions and at times comb through texts looking for the answer. Reading and combing through texts will not result in "finding" answers, but it is a great way to start the practice of asking questions and identifying topics of interest. It is also an opportunity to take notes on what questions have been researched and what scholars think need to be researched. This last is often found in sections of journal articles under implications or when scholars mention the limitations of the current research. In most dissertations, there is a future research section that points to research that is yet to be done that relates to the writer's current research. Looking at dissertations and articles on your own topics of interest can generate ideas that can be refined into topics and questions for your own research.

Personal Experience as a Starting Point for Research: Pros and Cons

Should qualitative researchers research issues with which they are personally acquainted and have personal experience? How advisable is it to conduct research in one's own profession, or at the place where one works, for example? Researchers are divided on this issue and, while no one right answer exists, those new to qualitative research might want to consider some issues pertaining to power and "insider" research and the difficulty of making "the familiar strange."

For example, if an elementary school principal wanted to conduct research in his own school and to find out to what extent teachers were engaged in the practice of culturally responsive teaching, he would perhaps find that teachers are eager to tell him what he wants to hear. Since this type of research would entail the principal spending time in classrooms, it may make teachers anxious about being judged and evaluated, even if the principal's intent is research and not evaluation. The issues of power need to be considered carefully since the principal will have greater power than a teacher. Similarly, if an employee at a large firm wanted to conduct research on the practices of leaders in the firm, it would present difficulties of access since the employee would have less power than the leaders in the firm. This represents a case of "studying up" and, while it is important to examine structures of power, the position of the researcher vis-à-vis the participant's changes and the researcher may not hold power. In these situations, the researcher may receive "canned" speeches, be offered a tour of the firm's showcased activities, and find herself unable to get at the issues she might want to explore. Those in favor of researching topics with which the researcher is personally acquainted argue that there is a driving force that propels such research, making it intense and valuable to the researcher. Cancer survivors, for example, have contributed valuable information on the social and psychological aspects of cancer and its treatment that have in turn influenced health science and caregiving. Those who argue against conducting such research raise doubts regarding how well the research can be conducted. What degree of bias will be present in the research? In contrast, in qualitative research, the researcher admits bias and uses it as a strength; if such positionality and reflexivity are not engaged, the researcher might not be able to see beyond what they would like to see. Or take, for example, the case of a student who wanted to study, from the perspective of a parent of children in special education, the experiences of students in special education, and who was angry and upset to discover that, contrary to her expectation, the students enjoyed school and their classes.

Research arising from personal experience can sometimes be undertaken because of "convenience" of access. Most researchers caution against topics that are "convenient" without careful thought to larger significance and personal meaning. Guba and Lincoln (2005) have suggested that topics have "educative authenticity" as a way to ensure depth. In terms of topics for qualitative research, studies that challenge taken-for-granted assumptions may be more significant than studies that seek to confirm such assumptions and may instead lead to trivial answers that lack depth (Bordage and Dawson, 2003). A question that lacks sufficient complexity and logic is not likely to garner support from committees or faculty. Scholars from a variety of fields (Crumley and Koufogiannakis, 2002 {Lib science}) agree that asking a good question is not easy and requires more effort and thinking than one might initially suppose. The fact that a research question is important can stymie some student researchers and lead to a sense of paralysis. The pressure to ask a good question can ironically prevent you from taking on a questioning and reflexive attitude, one that can spur you to ask questions and be reflexive.

In this chapter we discuss how we can develop good questions by refining and revising any initial questions or curiosities that we may generate at the outset of a project. The following two exercises are designed to stimulate your own thinking regarding your experiences and their links to possible research questions. The second exercise reminds you to consider the role of being an insider or outsider in your research project.

Try It Out: Research Journal Exercise 2.1

In your journal, use the following prompts to think about some experiences that have triggered questions or concerns for you that can lead to research.

1) What are some memories that stand out emotionally?
2) What questions do you have about those memories or incidents?
3) Looking back, what do you think those incidents were about?
4) Did you personally experience the incident or were you a bystander?
5) What questions arise for you today that might be linked to your research interests?

Try It Out: Research Journal Exercise 2.2

1) Where is the event or phenomenon you wish to investigate occurring?
2) Is this the best place to research the topic?

3) What do you know about the people/participants and the place? How familiar are you with the people and place?
4) Are you in a position of power or authority vis-à-vis the participants in your study?
5) How will you overcome the barriers that may result from your pre-existing relationship?
6) If you have no prior relationship with participants, whose side will you be on? Whose perspective do you wish to privilege or centralize?
7) How important is it to gather your data at this site with these participants?
8) Is this choice of sample and site based on convenience or research design?

Developing Research-Worthy Questions

Questions can serve as reflective tools to determine to what extent the topic is worthy of research or to what extent the topic is timely. Tracy (2010) addresses the question of what is a "worthy topic" Tracy, p. 839 and sheds light on how good qualitative research questions emerge.

According to Tracy, "Good qualitative research is relevant, timely, significant, interesting, or evocative" Tracy, p. 840. Researchers need to make decisions in order to figure out which questions can trigger research, or which questions are researchable questions. In order for topics to turn into issues or questions that are researchable, the theoretical framework, context, participants, methods for gathering data, and data analysis all need to be determined.

There are numerous ways to arrive at research-worthy questions, as is evidenced by the experiences of Alice Goffman (2014) and Sudhir Venkatesh (2008). Goffman's research questions were the product of her living in the neighborhood where she saw young men constantly "on the run" while Venkatesh's research emerged from a significant encounter with a person who would become his key participant or, in ethnographic terms, his key informant.

Alice Goffman (2014)'s journey into documenting the lives of young Black men "on the run" started with a broad interest to "understand the lives of . . . fellow workers at home and in the neighborhood" (p. 384). The second was her focus on "the problem of literacy" (p. 384), an interest born of her experiences as a cafeteria worker, where she saw her fellow Black workers use elaborate tactics to cover up their literacy deficiencies. However, pursuing her interest and living in a neighborhood which was, for her, "away" rather than representative of "home" led her to becoming curious and interested in learning more about the lives of young men who were constantly avoiding and dodging law enforcement officers as they navigated the complex, interrelated world of incarceration, bail, criminal activities, lawyers, judges, and the police as well as their extended families, girl-friends, and rival gangs.

Sudhir Venkatesh (2008) turned to ethnographic research when he saw the stark difference between his forays into the living, breathing city of Chicago and the Chicago that he saw in dry tables, statistics, and reports. Although he was not averse to the latter, he wanted to learn more than could be learned by sitting in a "classroom all day" (p. 30). He knocked on William Julius Wilson's door and returned with a survey instrument that he modified to learn how young Blacks were "affected by specific neighborhood factors" (p. 31). Venkatesh wandered into one of the project buildings only to be mistaken for a rival gang member and was held hostage for a day and night before the leader, J.T., let him go with some research advice on how to learn about young Black men:

> You shouldn't go around asking them silly-ass questions . . . with people like us, you should hang out, get to know what they do and how they do it. No one is going to answer questions like that. You need to understand how young people live on the streets.
>
> (p. 61)

Venkatesh took at him at his word and when J.T. offered him the chance to hang out with his gang, he saw his chance to learn from the inside how youth lived on the streets. In Venkatesh's case and in the case of Goffman, the desire to know was harnessed into a question that allowed them to examine issues that would make a contribution to the field of urban studies.

Devault (1990) approached the question of topics for research from a feminist perspective. She cautioned that discipline-specific topics (for example, from sociology) may or may not fit into the experiences that a researcher might want to explore. Instead, she advocated that researchers open up standard topics in ways that will allow for creative exploration. For example, she explained that her own interest in the study of housework or the work of providing food (or as she eventually came to refer to it, "feeding the family") did not quite fit into any particular topic construct. Such topics may be messy or controversial and resist neat classifications or definitions. Other feminist researchers (Stanko, 1985) also initiated research that defied topic categorization. Stanko (1985) examined the "strategic maneuvers" that women engage in to avoid assault or violence. These included making choices regarding what to wear and the paths to avoid while walking home or when to go to the laundromat. Devault's (1990) point is that it is important to create new topics that will contribute to knowledge and theory. We present a practice exercise that scholars can try out that will help clarify doubts and increase confidence at the starting point.

Try It Out: Research Journal Exercise 2.3

Questions that Researchers Can Pose to Themselves that Aid the Process of Designing Research

Ask yourself the following questions:

1) Why am I doing this study? or Why do I want to do this study?
2) What is interesting about it? or What is compelling to me about it? What might be compelling to others about it?
3) Why am I doing this at this moment in time? What contexts am I aware of and/or a part of that make this topic important to me?
4) How ready do I feel (emotionally, enthusiasm level, commitment level) to do this study?
5) What does the literature offer? What are the questions and/or bodies of knowledge related to this topic?

The above exercise allows you to think about your topic of interest in depth and ascertains to what extent you are ready to begin the process and what thinking or work you still need to do to be better prepared.

Researchers often wonder how to evaluate questions related to their research. Are all questions good questions? How can we develop good questions? Is it possible to distinguish between good questions and questions that may need further development or reflection? Scholars have discussed these issues and have suggested that good questions have some key characteristics that can be identified.

Good Questions Allow for Adaptation and Modification

Creswell pointed out that our questions change "during the process of research to reflect an increased understanding of the problem" (Creswell, 2007, p. 43). Such changes can emerge from researchers' understanding of their own roles, positionality, and perception of power relations vis-à-vis the participants'. Therefore good research questions may need to be modified, tweaked, or sometimes wholly rewritten in order to adjust to the realities of the iterative data-analysis process.

Good Questions Are Answerable

Research questions need data to be aligned with the questions so that the data needed to effectively answer/respond to the research questions can be gathered. How should such data be accessed? Can this research be completed within the time frame you have allotted for the study? Is the study designed to fit this scale? Sometimes a research question can be too ambitiously conceptualized and may need to be reframed in order to make it a "doable" or manageable project.

Good Questions Are Framed as Questions to Which We Do Not Yet Know the Answer

At times, students formulate questions that are of interest to them and, when probed deeper, they admit that they think they have an answer to the question already. This can influence the way they construct their research question that can ignore some significant areas of exploration. By adopting a mindset of wanting to learn and figure out a puzzle, researchers can keep themselves open to formulating questions that might lead them to new vistas.

Developing good research questions requires a mindset about the nature of the interactive process it entails. Asking and developing questions requires a dialogue with the self and with peer researchers. Peers can serve as a mirror to the self and can serve as catalysts, providing the stimulus for researchers to ask different types of questions. Peers can also help question assumptions that may be inherent in the research question yet difficult for you to see on your own. In addition, they can help the researcher to refine the question and figure out the direction of the research. Asking research questions has been considered both an important and yet difficult undertaking. Several models exist that can guide researchers in the formulation of good questions within different fields.

Models as Guides for Research Questions

In the medical field, several frameworks exist (PICO, Spice) that serve to remind one of the different stakeholders or processes that researchers need to keep in mind while formulating questions. For example, PICO stands for patient, intervention, comparison, and outcomes. This framework has been adapted for evidence-based practice in disciplines such as library science, which has used the PICO model to stand for population, intervention as a new concept, comparison, and outcomes. Several scholars have created variations on the model (Petticrew and Roberts, 2008; Schardt, Adams, Owens, Keitz and Fontelo, 2007) and SPICE was specifically created to answer questions in library science (Booth, 2007). The SPICE model has been developed for evidence-based practice and stands for setting, perspective, intervention, comparison, and evaluation.

In qualitative research, we can adapt these frameworks to keep in mind researcher roles and responsibilities as well as the different stakeholders and processes. We offer a model based on our experiences for qualitative research that comprises the five Ps of question generation. These are:

> Participants: Who are the people or participants in the research process?
>
> Places: Where will the research be undertaken?
>
> Perspective: What is the perspective or theory guiding the research question?
>
> • What is the perspective you adopt as a researcher?
>
> Phenomena: What phenomenon is being researched?
>
> Purpose: What is the purpose of the research?

Try out using this model to generate some questions for a research project.

Try It Out: Research Journal Exercise 2.4

Find a news article on a topic of interest. Using the above model, think about a research question that is based on what you have read.

1. Create a table or a diagram that encapsulates the above model. Use an image that helps you connect the different aspects of the model. This could be a tree, for example, or a brick house or a flowing river.
2. Write a few lines about how the process of creating a diagram on the model supported you to generate questions for research.

While these models can serve as signposts that guide question formulation, it is important for qualitative researchers to learn to distinguish between practitioners' questions and researchers' questions. Booth (2006, p. 365) offers a way to differentiate between the two by describing the former as questions focused on "what we know we don't know" versus questions focused on "what we don't know we don't know." For the latter, we would need to pay attention to taken-for-granted assumptions or routine actions that are carried out unquestioningly. In order to formulate questions that are research worthy, one way might be to keep a list of questions already studied in one's field or topic area and questions that still need exploration or further study.

Try it Out: Research Journal Exercise 2.5

1. Read five articles on your topic of interest.
2. Create a table of the questions that the authors studied.
3. In the same table, think of questions that another researcher in the same setting and context might have studied given all the information you have.
4. Look at the findings and the discussion sections of the article and see if there are any ideas or suggestions for future research.

Distinguishing between Research Questions (RQs) and Other Questions along the Research Journey

Research questions can be regarded as navigational tools that will guide the researcher during the journey and help map different pathways to investigate. Imaginative journeys can help formulate new ways of thinking about the research and generate new questions. If we imagine the researcher to be cartographer or an archeologist, we can picture how the researcher might approach questions along the research journey.

The researcher as cartographer: As a cartographer, a researcher needs to map different possibilities along the research journey. Such a role allows the researcher to respond to the unexpected that can occur in the field and make necessary changes to questions along the way.

In the role of cartographer, the researcher also reflects on questions and reformulates them and uses them as central points in navigating the research journey. This role allows the researcher to reflect on and assess whether or not decisions made at different points in the journey are appropriate.

In addition, cartography involves conceptualizing and creating "maps." Cartography practices parallel the work of researchers as we conceptualize concept maps, data maps, place and site-based maps, etc. What follows is a new set of questions we can generate based on the organizational patterns of the maps we cobble together as organizers or representations of our thought processes related to qualitative inquiry.

The researcher as archeologist: Since qualitative questions are always evolving, if we imagine the researcher to be an archeologist, we can remain cognizant of how new discoveries may lead to new questions. Initial questions may be exploratory while later questions may be based on early observations in the field. Archeology is excavating material culture and piecing together clues worthy of further interrogation. Thinking about how a researcher may operate as an archaeologist focuses our attention on the kinds of questions we can generate from the material remains surrounding our studies.

Asking Qualitative Questions: A Starting Point

Janesick (2000, p. 382) suggests beginning with the question: What do I want to know in this study? whereas Charmaz (2006, p. 20) suggests broad questions such as: What are the basic social processes? Wolcott suggests even broader questions such as: What is going on here? Maxwell (2005, p. 65) refers to these questions as provisional questions while pointing out that even early questions are indicative of the direction of theory and methods. Agee (2009) points out that initial questions generated by novice researchers are likely to be too broad and lacking a reference point to a particular context. Richardson and Wilson (1997) distinguish questions asked by novices, or researchers new to the field, from those asked by an experienced researcher within the field. They refer to the former as "background" questions and the latter as "foreground" questions. They explain that prior knowledge influences and determines the types of questions researchers pose. Since qualitative research is about particular people, places, or experiences of people and how they might interpret them, Agee (2009) suggests a dialogic process to move researchers from an overly broad perspective to more focused questions. Therefore, qualitative research questions need to get at descriptions and good qualitative questions cannot be answered with a "yes" or a "no." As the study progresses, qualitative questions are likely to become more focused; however, as Maxwell warns, questions that are too focused lead researchers into the danger of "tunnel vision" (Maxwell, 2005, p. 67).

Maxwell explains that research questions need to account for one's "tentative theories about phenomena" (Maxwell, 2005, p. 68), while others believe that research questions should be regarded as signposts that will provide information on the type of study, the concepts, the assumptions, the participants, and the context (Strauss and Corbin, 1998). Eldredge (2002) explained that questions can be either predictive or exploratory and characterized exploratory questions as appropriate for qualitative research. Such questions may ask "why" or ask a question that reveals unintended consequences of an intervention. For example, Booth (2006) described that while initial training of database use abated anxiety of users, further training paradoxically increased anxiety. To explore why this was the case, researchers would need to ask a qualitative exploratory question.

Mantzoukas (2008) suggests that qualitative questions need to have three elements: content, coherence, and structure. By content, he refers to the context of the question or area of interest. The researcher would narrate the personal biographical connections to the research question and the observations or contradictions that led to the research questions. In addition, research questions should be qualitative and not veer off into quantitative questions. Such questions need not necessarily be stated as an interrogative sentence and can instead be declarative. They should be prefaced with a why or a how rather than a "how much." A qualitative question needs to strike a balance by not being too focused or too broad. By being too focused, the researcher runs into the hazard of imposing preconceived ideas by creating leading questions. By being too broad, it may prevent the reader from figuring out whether or not the research questions have been answered. Research questions can be more focused than the topic but less so than the specific questions for interviewees. By coherence, he means that the research question needs to be aligned with a research paradigm. The question needs to reflect the ideas of the paradigm and link them to the approaches or the type of study that will be undertaken by the researcher. These would include types of studies such as phenomenological studies or narrative studies, or interpretive, critical, or feminist approaches. With regard to structure, research questions should contain the answer to questions viz. the who, what, when, where, how, and why of the study.

Selecting a Theoretical Framework to Inform Research Questions

Are qualitative research designs set in stone like blueprints in architecture with little room to make changes or like a contract that cannot be broken without penalties? Or can qualitative research designs be regarded as outline sketches that need to be finessed and filled in and worked on during the process of research? Terms, such as "theoretical integration" (Corbin and Strauss, 2015) and "methodological congruence" (Morse and Richards, 2002), refer to the interconnected nature of research questions to the purpose of the study and the methods used to pursue the research questions.

Some scholars, such as Yin (1994), suggest that a theoretical framework is needed to inform research questions. Questions can point to theory explicitly or implicitly. Maxwell (2005, p. 68) explains that research questions need to account for one's "tentative theories about phenomena."

While questions can be formulated around theories explicitly, theory can be implicitly present in research questions, leading researchers towards particular theories for their work. The purpose of research can indicate the theoretical framework and, conversely, the theoretical framework can hint at the type of question to ask. A research question that has to do with teacher empowerment can be formulated within several frameworks. In a post-positivist framework, the question could be: How are best practices aligned with the policies on teacher empowerment in school districts? Within an interpretivist framework, the question would be refocused as: How do teachers and administrators define teacher empowerment? Or what are teachers' and administrators' perspectives of empowerment? The focus would be on the meaning or on their interpretation of empowerment. A critical framework would involve questions of power and the research question could be recast as: How does the status or power of teachers change or shift with empowerment? A feminist framework might include the question: How do women teachers who are empowered make meaning of empowerment? What are teachers' narratives of empowerment? In the following exercise, try out creating questions that reflect different theoretical frameworks.

Try it Out: Research Journal Exercise 2.6

The goal of this exercise is to practice formulating questions from different lenses.

1. Read a research article in your area of interest. Find the research question.
2. What is the theoretical framework of the research question?
3. Are there other clues in the article that give you a sense of the author's use of a particular theoretical perspective?
4. Reframe the question within three different theoretical frameworks.
5. What do you notice happens once you change the question to align with the framework?
6. What are some challenges this exercise posed and what did you do to overcome those challenges?

If we acknowledge that research questions need to be focused and yet broad enough to allow for adaptation in the field, questions in the field further inform research questions and in turn data collection.

Data Collection Questions

Data collection is a broad umbrella term encompassing the process from selecting participants, sites, and times of data collection. The process of selecting participants and sites is referred to as sampling strategy and is determined by several factors.

Sampling Questions and Strategies

Sampling is often glossed over in qualitative methodology texts as it is usually treated as a procedure that yields participants for research. However, qualitative sampling is a complex process which is tied to the purpose of the research and involves subtle forms of decision-making. Sampling decisions reflect the researcher's theoretical perspective, methodological approach, and positionality or interpretive stance. Purposeful sampling is generally used in qualitative research. The type of sample used within qualitative research might be different depending on the topic of research. Sampling is a method by which the researcher identifies participants, organizations, or research settings appropriate to the research study. The researcher makes this determination by asking what site/sites will shed light on a particular phenomenon or whose experience most closely aligns with what the researcher wants to explore. Criteria for determining who should participate in a study is usually part of the sampling process. Sampling in qualitative research is typically focused on small sampling sizes, in contrast with quantitative sampling. The argument for a small sample in qualitative research is to allow for depth in the study. In qualitative research, sampling is done purposefully so that information-rich samples are selected that illuminate the issue or question that the researcher is trying to understand. There are different types of sampling that scholars have discussed:

Intensity sampling: Intensity sampling typically comprises small sample sizes. For example a small group is interviewed several times in order to get in-depth information and stories.

Snowball sampling: Snowball sampling is used for difficult-to-access populations. In cases where groups are difficult to access, asking for referrals from participants can result in a robust sample size.

Typical/negative case/atypical or exemplary case: At times, a researcher can learn lessons from a negative case or an exemplary case. This would involve looking for cases that are unusual—a case of a dramatic failure or success. Case studies can be of a group as well as that of individuals, depending on the research study. One way to consider sampling in qualitative research is to ask: What case or cases will best illuminate the problem or issue I am researching? If that case is an atypical case, and is appropriate to the issue, it is important to take it up for study. For example, survivors and those who have overcome adverse circumstances are often broached as atypical cases worthy of study to understand what made the exceptions possible. Similarly, case studies of academically successful schools with students who are from high-poverty neighborhoods and families are studied to understand the conditions that create such success.

Grounded theory and theoretical sampling: Unlike other sampling strategies mentioned above, theoretical sampling takes place later in the study. In studies employing grounded theory, theoretical sampling (Charmaz, 2000) is used to refine ideas during the process of analysis. Therefore, if a theory is emerging from the analysis, the researcher may want to clarify concepts emerging from the data with participants, leading to a second interview. It may also lead researchers to re-enter settings or contexts to examine it further for a confirmation or explanation of the analysis.

Sampling in case studies: In case studies two types of sampling strategies need to be clarified: the selection of the case and the selection of participants within the case (Merriam, 1998; Patton, 2002). In addition, selection of sites is also part of the process of sampling.

Amanda Lewis (2005) explains her rationale for choosing California as the state in which to explore issues of race. Demographic changes in California have kept the issues of diversity front and center. Race-related policies have generated controversy (Proposition 187, 209) and, finally, California's race relations exemplify a diversity that goes beyond the Black/White politics and are prescient of what is to come in other parts of the United States. She chose Hillside as the town in which to do research because it was a city where there was "extensive interracial interaction" (p. 198). Mueller and Buckley (2014) describe sampling strategies and participants in the following way: "We recruited 20 'active' fathers of children with disabilities using purposeful sampling" (p. 42). They go on to explain their criteria for recruiting fathers into the study as fathers who had a child with a disability and, in addition, were "active" in terms of "attending IEP meetings, parent-teacher conferences, and the ability to speak about multiple interactions with the child's educators" (p. 42). Sampling strategies are tied to the purpose of the study and to the methodological approach and are not neutral choices. They are influenced by the positionality of the researcher and the sociocultural context of the research.

Final choices of site and participants are often made keeping in mind not only external criteria that meet the needs of the study but also internal criteria not often voiced by the researcher. Lewis (2005), for example, describes her process for narrowing down her choices for a typical urban school site for her research. She used external criteria to determine which sites presented possibilities. She began by eliminating those schools that had special programs that made them unique as sites that were not "typical." Next, since her focus was on race issues, she chose schools that had large populations of Blacks and Latinos. She eliminated schools that were under threat of closure or reconstitution since those schools were likely to be facing different types of challenges. She found five schools and then narrowed down the selection further to two. Both schools satisfied her external sampling criteria. At this point, she visited both schools and made her final selection. Her final selection was made on her perception regarding which principal appeared to be more interested in her presence and research. In her words, "In the end, I selected West City Elementary because . . . in my meetings with her, the West City principal seemed interested in having me there rather than just being tolerant of my presence" (p. 199). Internal criteria such as comfort level with "gatekeepers" (in this case, the leadership at the site) also play a significant role in sampling choices.

Researchers need to keep in mind two sets of questions while making sampling choices. These are given below and can be used as practice exercises for your research journal.

Try It Out: Research Journal Exercise 2.7

A.   What are the *external criteria* I am using to narrow down site/participant choices?

   1.   How do these external criteria meet the needs of my research question, purpose statement, and research design?

   2.   Whom am I leaving out and why?

   3.   Who is being included and why?

   4.   What is determining my choice of place or site for the research?

   5.   What alternatives exist and what are my reasons for my choices?

B.   What are the *internal criteria* I am using to make my final choices?

   1.   What is my comfort level in the field and with participants?

   2.   What is making me anxious about entering the field?

   3.   What is exciting me about entering the field and starting data gathering?

   4.   What other emotions am I feeling as I prepare for my first interview/observation?

   5.   Is this the best sampling strategy to get at the purpose of my study?

Questions regarding internal criteria may not surface until one has been in contact with participants or the site in question. However, this is an important methodological note to make to allow one to reflect on the choices being made.

Although there are no strict rules regarding particular sampling strategy that need to be utilized with specific methodological approaches, there is no doubt that some align more closely than others. If the researcher wants to explore the lived experiences of a particular group of people or phenomenon, the researcher needs to ensure that all participants identify with that group and have actually had that experience (e.g., first-year teachers, parents of terminally ill children, gay-bisexual college students' experiences of higher education). Therefore, the researcher needs to begin with intensity sampling or ensuring that all participants selected meet the criteria. In a case study, after appropriate selection of cases, a further strategy may be to decide whether the cases should represent maximum variation or minimum variation, negative cases, or atypical or typical cases. In other words, the purpose of the study will determine additional criteria to create a boundary around the sample or limit it. As the researcher, you will have to justify the sampling strategy to argue that this is the best method to get at the purpose of the study. Therefore the researcher has to select a strategy and then justify it by arguing that it is the best method to get at the purpose of the study.

Troubleshooting Sampling Issues

At times, it may be difficult to access certain groups that one wants to study. For example, accessing early school leavers or pushouts from school to find out what experiences led them to leave school without graduating is not easy because the potential participants cannot be found in school but in the community. Some of them may not want to be found and others may not want to divulge their lack of a diploma. What does one do if participants do not want to discuss what the researcher wants to know more about? In such cases the research design can be reconsidered. In cases where the topics are sensitive and few people want to discuss them, case studies or life histories may allow for in-depth knowledge.

The following exercise can stimulate thinking around issues of sampling and strategies of rapport building, as well as help guide the writing of an initial memo that outlines your thinking process.

Try It Out: Research Journal Exercise 2.8

Questions to Guide Selection of Participants and Gaining Access to Them

1. Have I conveyed my interest in the phenomenon to the participants?
2. Have I conveyed my knowledge of the phenomenon to the participants?
3. Am I looking for participants who are usually not included in this type of study?
4. Am I unwittingly further marginalizing my participants by incorporating a single diverse participant, a participant with an opposing point of view?
5. Are participants who represent differing perspectives adequately represented?
6. Why would participants want to participate in my study?
7. Do I have any incentives to offer them?
8. What will participants get out of the relationship/research partnership?
9. Can I develop any form of reciprocity in the field?
10. What type of study am I doing? Is it using a feminist or participatory action methodology—and if so, have I considered that participants need to contribute to the research design and questions?
11. Have I thought about my own socially constructed identity?

    - How do I identify and how am I perceived?
    - Will my identity/identities impact (positively or negatively) my ability to establish rapport or trust?

Once participants have been identified, and the research context determined, data collection can begin. Between the stages of determining participants and data collection is the application for approval of research from the Institutional Review Board (IRB). While it is not our intent to give a full account of the IRB process here, we would like to make a few points related to researcher positionality about the importance of questions related to consent in this regard.

So far we have discussed the different ways in which questions and question generation can serve as a tool for critical thinking and creativity. We have also discussed critical approaches as challenging the status quo by focusing on the concealed, invisible, marginalized, or omitted topics, people, and spaces of research. Informing participants of what their role is in the research project is an accepted ethical practice in qualitative research. Often this process of informed consent is reduced to the researcher giving a short summary of the research and asking for permission to record the interview or observe the event. A simple "yes" is all that is required for what is often deemed a formality to be completed. However, we wish to point out that informed consent allows a space for questioning by the participants beyond the formality of consent. This information and communication to the participants allows them to question the researcher so that the researcher has an opportunity to engage in a relationship in which the position of power is held by the participants, even if temporarily, as they hold the power of access. In other contexts (for example, in international contexts), the researcher may find that the power to consent may not apply, as some participants may not understand the academic contexts of research. In such cases, it is the researcher who relies on reflexivity to make decisions about the ethics of research and data collection. In several countries, ethics committees do not require clearance for interviews and focus groups and only for invasive intervention in health-related fields. Qureshi (2010) describes research in Pakistan, where she decided to tell the participants that she was writing for a newspaper as a way to help the participants understand the activities she would be undertaking. In her view, "this is not deception, but the right kind of information for participants to understand the purpose of our activities if not the purpose of our research" (p. 83). It is our contention that, for international and cross-cultural research which we have experience with, the research responsibility lies with the researcher in determining the extent of harm or exposure to risk in which participants might unwittingly place themselves. A good rule of thumb for researchers is to imagine the impact of the research on the lives of participants, given that participants stay and continue to live on after the research is concluded in what researchers often refer to as the "field," while they themselves exit. Overall, our point in this section is for researchers to remain alert to their own position of power and privilege in the research endeavor. In the next section, we move to examining interviews.

Interviews and Interview Questions

Interviews are complex interactions that require the researcher to simultaneously engage in listening, recording, thinking of follow-up questions, figuring out what to pursue and what to back away from, and working through the general direction of the interview. Interview questions follow from the type of interview that researchers set up. These can have rigid structures, be very flexible, or find a happy medium. Typically, qualitative interviews are semi-structured or, at times, unstructured. Scholars point out that even so-called unstructured interviews have an underlying structure to them (Mason, 2002). Completely unstructured interviews could lead researchers to run the risk of getting superficial accounts of experiences (Price, 2002). Regardless of the structure of the interview, qualitative interviews tend to have open-ended questions. Open-ended questions are questions that elicit descriptive answers, stories, and experiences from participants. They cannot be answered with a "yes" or "no." Therefore some general rule of thumb questions to ask yourself while formulating interview questions would be:

1. Does the interview begin with a "grand tour" (Spradely, 1979) question? This type of approach centers on a general question to the participant related to the central research question.
2. Does the interview have "throwaway" questions (Berg, 2008)? These would be questions that establish initial comfort through a personal greeting approach and help with building a connection that may or may not yield usable data. Examples are, "How was your day?" or a question about the weather.
3. Do the interview questions relate to the research question?

4. Will the interview questions yield a conversation that will be pertinent to the research?

5. Is there enough room for the interview to follow the lead of the participant if necessary?

6. Does the interview close with a question that allows participants to add information? Some examples would be: Is there anything you would like to add to what you have said so far? Have I neglected to ask questions about something you think I should have asked? Is there anything else you think I should know about this issue?

7. What is my stance vis-à-vis the participant? Have I thought through my own emotional response to the participant? Is there a rapport or empathetic connection that I can maintain that is authentic to the degree possible?

8. What is my stance vis-à-vis the content of what the participant is going to say? Have I thought about how to respond if I hear something I do not like? Have I found a way to remain neutral through the interview process?

9. Can I maintain a sense of empathy with the participant while maintaining a sense of neutrality with regard to the content of what I hear?

In formulating questions, besides figuring out what those interview questions might be and how they relate to the research questions, it is also important to keep in mind the position of the researcher vis-à-vis the participant.

Interviews as Conversations or Reciprocal Interviewing

Devault (1990) moved away from the form, vocabulary, and structure of traditional interviews to an informal conversation mode that at times caused her respondents to question, "Is this really what you want? Are you sure this is helping you?" (p. 99). Devault (1990) points out that merely thinking about open-ended questions for interviewing does not always get at useful accounts. This is especially true for non-dominant members of society who are used to interpreting their experiences in the language used and meanings attributed by the dominant society. The responsibility of the researcher, in such cases, is to ground interviews in ways that will be more like "woman talk" (Smith, 1987, p. 187–189).

Several scholars (Price, 2002) remind us that interviewing participants involves more than receiving information. It is a process where meaning is co-created between the researcher or interviewer and the participant being interviewed and centers on the meaning and sense-making of participants' experiences. They also remind us that research interviews involve issues of power and are not social conversations. It is important therefore to remember that researchers have power over the way the questions are prioritized and in addition the power to bring back respondents to the agenda if they deviate from it. The interviewer has been likened to a detective (Fontana and Frey, 2000) who is looking for pertinent information.

Although many scholars have written about the impact of the power relations between the researcher and the participant and the importance of acknowledging the power difference, it can nevertheless be a taken-for-granted idea unless we can unpack what that means and in what ways the research interview may be compromised or limited by this power difference. Mishler (1986) argues that there is more power in the hands of the researcher, as participants often try to please the researcher with answers that might be their perception of "what the study requires." For example, in one of our research projects with high school students, the youth interviewed often inquired about the "length of the paper" and if they could "help." Pack (2006) points out that participants will often only reveal what they want the researcher to know even if they are answering a prepared set of questions. For interviews, researchers often have to think on their feet in order to maintain the pace of the interview. Researchers also have to think through how to probe or ask further questions in a manner that sustains the interview process. It is possible for interviewees to feel like they are either being threatened or praised and therefore either clam up or offer more in-depth information on a particular subset of questions. Therefore, a question for researchers to reflect on while formulating interview questions, or preparing for the interview, is to think about how to ask more questions about a topic without making the interview seem like an interrogation. Some typical qualitative interview follow-up questions, or probes, have been described by scholars (Bernard, 2000). Here, however, we have used typical follow-up questions and probes from our own research projects.

Typical Probes for Interviews

1. Can you tell me more about that?
2. Can you give me an example?
3. Am I understanding you correctly?
4. If I might summarize . . . Did I understand that properly?
5. Is there another story you recall that might illustrate what you mean?
6. How did that come to take place?
7. What do you wish had happened?
8. What if _____ had changed in the following ways?
9. What do you think is happening here?
10. Is there anything else you would like to share with me about . . .

The depth of the interview will depend on the rapport between the interviewer and participant. The unique perspective a researcher brings to the interview is a strength and should be capitalized on, as it directly contributes to the dialogic interpretations that follow.

Rapport Building with Participants for Interviews

Different paradigms within qualitative research have different expectations with regard to the researcher and participant roles. In the positivist paradigm there is considerable separation and distance between the researcher and the participant, while in the critical or feminist paradigms, that separation is considered antithetical to equity and power-sharing concerns. Pack's (2006) description of his initial introduction to Navajo culture and the Benally family points to the importance of approaching communication and rapport building tentatively. Pack was quiet, not particularly gregarious or outgoing, and while these attributes often earned him the title of being stand-offish in mainstream culture, it happened to fit into Navajo culture perfectly. The Navajos he met were less suspicious of him and more accepting, as he let the relationship and rapport develop slowly rather than trying to force it. Pack's descriptions of his time in the Navajo family are especially important for qualitative researchers because he represents a unique example. Pack was not only a researcher, but was often mistaken for a Navajo himself. Although he was Korean-American, his features were often taken to be Indian and, as a result, he was in the unique position of experiencing both what it felt like to be a participant or recruited as a participant while being a researcher himself. Often other researchers from universities would try to recruit him to be a participant and allowed him to see what that approach felt like from the Navajo perspective. His words remind us of the importance of the communication with participants and the reason to practice reflexivity often. He says, "with their overly polite manner of speaking, exaggerated enunciation of words, and friendly body language, I can best compare this treatment to the way adults speak to retarded children" (Pack, p. 108). Pack's differing roles in his work with Navajos and his movement from being regarded as an outsider to an insider teaches us that both roles come with opportunities and limitations. As an outsider he could move freely from family to family and not engage in inter-family rivalry or squabbles, but as an insider he was unwittingly placed on one side or the other in such squabbles and his research with one family meant he inherited their relationship dynamics with other members of the clan. Perhaps the best lesson we can learn from Pack's experiences is that, as researchers, we are interpreted and observed by participants as much as we observe and interpret our participants and their activities.

Some points while setting up interviews can impact the extent of power sharing that occurs between the interviewer and participant as well as the quality of the data gathered. As qualitative interviewers, we like to be aware of the subtle power dynamics that may be at play when setting up interviews. For example, how does the space where interviews will take place get agreed upon? Who suggests the spaces? How comfortable is it for the participant? While the intention of rapport building and power sharing on the part of qualitative researchers is important to carry out, it is also important for us to remember that from a reflexive point of view, rapport building and making participants comfortable are all moves that benefit the researcher and the research study (Glesne and Peshkin, 1992). To this extent, qualitative researchers need to acknowledge, without getting paralyzed, that the power dynamics between the researcher and participants are most often weighted in favor of the researcher. Rapport is the "ability to convey empathy and understanding without judgment" (Patton, 2002, p. 366).

Lewis (2005) gives an example of how she prepared for the language she would and would not use in interviews by observing what was appropriate in the setting and by trying out some potential interview questions in casual settings. For example, she observed that students often quizzed each other about identity through direct questions. One student asked another, "What are you?" to which he received the response, "Black and Creole." Another incident that made her aware of what terms she would use or not use took place when a substitute teacher referred to the term "race" and students asked her, "What is that?" (Lewis, 2005, p. 206).

Preparing to conduct interviews and formulate interview questions, as we can see from Lewis's (2005) case, requires an attention to language. Researchers, in addition, need to keep in mind their research questions even as they construct interview questions in order to make explicit the links between the two. It is at times possible in qualitative research that the research question itself needs modification or rewriting as the interview questions or fieldwork redirects the focus of the researcher. A practical tip for researchers is to create a table or chart where they write the research questions in one column and link them to interview questions in a second column.

Researcher as Listener/Sensory Awareness of Researchers

Learning to create good research questions, related interview questions, and self-posed reflexivity questions requires researchers to fine-tune their listening skills. In the field of language skills, listening has received short shrift and has often been relegated to a skill that one can master by osmosis (Mendelsohn, 1984; Oxford, 1993). Listening, often considered a passive skill, is rarely taught in courses in research methods. Spender (1980) attributes the neglect of listening in favor of speech to the power differential between those who air their views versus those who listen. She argued that members of subordinated groups learn to listen well since they have honed that skill. As Osada (2004) explains, listeners have to process speech at the speed determined by the speakers and it can be difficult to ask speakers to repeat what they said or explain it. Listening involves certain types of background knowledge. Goffman's (2014) experiences are a case in point. She explains her initial inability to understand not only the African American vernacular English, but also events and the context of conversations. She admits, "I was struggling to overcome a language barrier" (Goffman, 2014, p. 412). Goffman's struggles were, as she realized, not merely her own internal perception, but they were reinforced by her participants' bafflement at how slow she was to grasp what was going on. Goffman overcame this barrier with time, something that researchers who conduct short-term studies are unlikely to do. Instead, they run the danger of not quite grasping the social context within which such listening takes place. Goffman's account illustrates the difficulty of hearing things said in a language one is not used to. A similar difficulty can arise with the form and structure that one is used to. Riessman (1987) describes a case where an interviewer's difficulty in understanding an interviewee's episodic narrative style resulted in a disastrous interview as the interviewer repeatedly interrupted the participant to clarify chronology, timelines, and links between episodes and incidents.

In speaking of language differences, Devault (1990) does not refer to a different vernacular or dialect; instead she points out that the dominant "language itself reflects male experiences . . . it's categories are often incongruent with women's lives" (Devault, 1990, p. 96). However, rather than see this as a barrier, she argues that by paying attention to "research as activity fundamentally grounded in talk" (Devault, 1990, p. 97), this difference can be used as an advantage. Non-dominant groups often learn to "translate" their ideas and words into dominant language so that some parts of their voices become muted and need to be recovered by the researcher, who needs to practice deep listening, a listening that goes beyond words. Listening does not end with the interview session; if interviews are taped, researchers need to listen to the tapes, to study the transcripts. In her own research, Devault (1997) describes that she listened carefully to the halting, often inarticulate expressions of her participants. When her participants struggled to express a thought or a process, Devault became interested since she realized and later analyzed such moments as signaling the unacknowledged part of "food preparation" or of "providing for the family" in the dominant discourse available for such descriptions. She began to realize how the managerial term "planning" was not an adequate term to describe the processes with which the women engaged. She also realized that moments when her respondents said "you know" were times that were a request for understanding, a plea for the researcher to meet them halfway so that they could help to articulate what they themselves had difficulty expressing. If the researcher does understand and murmurs a "uh-huh" it is important for the researcher to unpack that shared moment and explain those thoughts.

Summarizing

In 1986 Wilen and Clegg published a brief article addressing social studies teachers within secondary education that provided a review of the literature regarding "Effective Questions and Questioning" (Wilen and Clegg, 1986) and developed a list of effective questioning practices for teachers. And in 1984, Werdmann and King developed some ways to think about how teachers can develop and analyze questions. We have borrowed the framing of both of these short pieces and developed the following list of effective questioning practices for qualitative researchers as a way of summarizing:

Effective Interview Questioning Practices for Qualitative Researchers

1. First, effective questioners must be effective listeners. For example, researchers need to learn to be comfortable with the use of "wait-time" when interviewing participants, using questions that require them to engage in higher-cognitive levels involving analysis, synthesis, and evaluation of their own ideas and/or expressions of understanding. Listening and questioning go hand in hand.

2. Questions must be phrased clearly.
3. Questions need to be related to the theoretical framing chosen for the study.
4. Some questions need to be designed specifically to help build rapport.
5. Questions ought to be designed to elicit both convergent and divergent thinking. Stay cognizant of the effects of open and closed questions. Open questions encourage divergent thinking and are more broad-based; additionally, more than one answer may arise within the participant's response. Closed questions encourage convergent thinking and a narrowing of possible responses.
6. Questions designed to elicit affect, feelings, and emotional responses are often needed. For example: How did you feel about that situation? What part made you feel that way? Can you describe how that made you feel? Can you tell me a bit more about how you were feeling at that time?
7. Questions can be designed to elicit application of certain types of thinking. Learning how participants apply their thinking to particular contexts, scenarios, and future situations can also assist with a researcher's desire to more deeply understand a participant's experiences.
8. Use questions to aid in clarification, probe ideas in more in-depth ways, stimulate nuanced thinking, and encourage transparent reflection.
9. Be aware of how the various questions you are operating with function within the overall study. Are they designed for interpretation? To elicit perceptions? To form the ground for analysis or evaluation? To increase or improve engagement?

Ethics and Research Questions

The effects of research questions when researching vulnerable populations is important to pay attention to since researchers represent the lives of vulnerable people and may not always know the long-term effects of such representation on their lives. Issues and questions regarding representation have led researchers to move towards more collaborative participatory research where research questions are developed in dialogue with participants.

Focus Group Questions

Kamberelis and Dimitriadis (2013) explain that focus groups have traditionally been utilized as interviews that are conducted in groups where the "focus" was more important than the "group."

By examining focus groups as a way to centralize the group, as well as to regard focus groups as a site for transformation, collective action, and the possibility of examining the self and other in different ways, they offer a different vision of the focus group and its possibilities. An emphasis on the "group" makes it possible for focus groups to be possible sites where learning and teaching can take place, or where solidarity can be established and where the selves can be "selves in dialogue, social selves and selves in community" (p. 21). Focus groups can be conducted in different ways, with some researchers using the setting to structure a conversation while others might leave it more open ended. The difference lies in how the focus group is conceptualized and the purpose of the focus group interview. Kamberelis and Dimitriadis (2013) caution researchers against using the focus group as a convenient tool or as a way to combine several individual interviews together. According to them focus groups should be "conceptualized as groups and not simply as collections of individuals" (p. 34).

Focus group questions require special consideration. Focus groups are conversations and dialogues with a group of people that can be focused around a set of predetermined questions prepared by the researcher who can also act as a facilitator. Focus groups may also be structured so that the researcher initiates the conversation with a few remarks and lets the group discuss their views and perspectives with little direction from the researcher. The researcher listens as the group continues their discussion. The role of the researcher is to facilitate the group discussion by periodically asking a follow-up question or a clarification. Yet, even this role needs to be somewhat muted in the focus group that has as its purpose not only to gather data but to promote a sense of solidarity among the group members.

An example of a researcher who changed how she approached focus groups and the questions she initially thought to ask was Simmons (2002) in her discussions with girls on bullying by girls in several ninth grade classrooms. Carrying with her a list of questions, she found them to be completely irrelevant as she listened while the girls "hooted, screeched, laughed, snorted, and veered off into personal stories, while notes flew around the room" (p. 5). She followed her instinct and abandoned carefully orchestrated conversations and let the girls lead where they wanted to go. In doing so, Simmons (2002) had an insight that most adult-led conversations on bullying were often strictures instructing girls not to engage in such behavior rather than allowing a free space for them to discuss the behaviors. Simmons (2002) countered this restricted conversational space by assuming that such acts were, in fact, occurring. By changing the way she facilitated these discussions, she allowed personal stories to emerge from the girls and for a sense of group solidarity to form as the girls realized they were not alone in their experiences. Another point that researchers using focus groups need to keep in mind is the question of confidentiality. Kamberelis and Dimitriadis (2013) point out that focus groups can be safe spaces where sensitive topics can be discussed and shared among a group while the same may feel threatening in an individual interview.

Overall, while researchers can decide what type of focus group they wish to form, they have choices depending on the context. Some contexts may be less conducive to a focus group while others may be more appropriate. In focus group interviews, the researcher needs to navigate permissions from the group so that issues of confidentiality can be worked out in advance. Since the researcher cannot guarantee that members of the focus group will not reveal their discussions to others, the group tends to find its balance depending on prior knowledge of each other and the dynamics of the group itself.

Researchers often have questions regarding the optimum numbers in a focus group and whether or not the group should be researcher led. While there is no "correct" answer to these questions, on the whole, a focus group works best when the group is large enough to generate discussion but not so large as to prevent full participation from everyone.

There are, however, some suggestions and questions that can help researchers who might wish to include focus groups as part of their data gathering efforts.

Questions that researchers need to keep in mind while considering focus groups:

1. How will the group be organized?
2. Who will the participants be?
3. Am I prepared to handle conflict in the group?
4. Am I prepared to facilitate group dynamics that may lead to one subset of people talking the most with others not participating?
5. What questions should I ask?

    a. Have I prepared a brief introduction that includes the description of the study and an invitation and acknowledgement of the groups participating?
    b. Have I prepared a list of questions, topics, and issues that the group can discuss?
    c. Did I try out the questions with a peer or a small group and revise the questions?
    d. How will I draw attention to the research questions in case a discussion veers off topic completely?
    e. How do I remain more muted and in the background so that the participants can take the lead in the discussions?

Moderating or facilitating the focus group can be practiced over time. The best way to acquire these skills is to try, if possible, to observe a focus group interview and then analyze it for what worked and what would have worked better. Moderators need to be prepared for differing opinions, conflictual points of view, and the possibility of a group arriving at a point of solidarity.

Try It Out: Research Journal Exercise 2.9

1. Think of two different ways in which focus groups can be organized: one with the researchers taking the lead and the other with the researcher remaining more or less in the

background. What are some implications for data gathering in each scenario?

2. Which scenario makes you feel more comfortable and why/ less comfortable and why?
3. What are some pros and cons with creating a space for solidarity through focus groups?

Questions to Aid the Process of Data Collection and Data Analyses

Qualitative researchers often ask: How much data is considered enough? How do I know when I can stop gathering data? Often these questions are dependent on the quality and quantity of data gathered in relation to the topic of the research. If the topic of research is one that few people have tackled so far, gathering less data may not pose problems while, for a topic that has been well researched, it may be necessary to gather more data to be able to generate differences in findings from previous research and to show nuances in the data gathered. If the researcher has been examining the data in the process of gathering it, s/he may be aware of what data still needs to be gathered and how much "data saturation" has occurred. Data saturation is a term used by scholars (Berg, 2008; Yin, 2011) when no new insights emerge from data or no new data is yielded from interviews, observations, or other data gathering methods in the field. Usually, data saturation is the marker used by researchers to stop gathering more data and turn to the process of iterative analysis. Questions that can guide the process of thinking through when data are enough are given below in Research Journal Exercise 2.10.

Try It Out: Research Journal Exercise 2.10

1. Did I spend enough time in the field?
2. Did I gather enough data?
3. How much raw data did I gather?
4. Did I gather data from all the participants?

5. How did I approach those who refused to participate at the first instance?
6. What is my strategy for reconnecting with participants for follow-up questions?
7. Are there other people in the field from whom I should have gathered data?
8. Did I get contexts into the data collection?
9. Did I gather different types of data appropriate to my questions?
10. Is there anything that I may have missed that I should have asked or observed?
11. In what ways are my data limited or incomplete?
12. What is my process for exiting the field?

Questions While Writing Fieldnotes

Writing fieldnotes on initial encounters with participants or with a new site is important. This is the time that most qualitative researchers use to describe their initial feelings, the contrasts between themselves and their participants, the similarities of interests, or what surprised them or the assumptions they made while entering the field. While these descriptions are useful, Judith Okley (1992) reminds us that the responses and insights from the participants or hosts on the site is much more important to capture and describe. She says, "In the long run it is important to know how they viewed and related to the anthropologist as stranger, guest, then apprentice, perhaps friend and scribe" (p. 14).

Fieldnotes comprise observation notes, reflections, and any questions and musings that the researcher might decide to add. They also contain drawings of settings, sketches of meetings that illustrate people at the table who can lead to a better understanding of power dynamics in meetings and maps of movement and stillness. It is easy to imagine a corridor of a school filled with movement while, during other times, it may be the parking lot that is filled with activity. Fieldnotes are jottings of the researcher and, as the examples above illustrate, how to take notes while in the field differs from one context to another. Although there appears to be a distinction between "doing fieldwork" and "writing fieldnotes," Emerson, Fretz and Shaw (2011) argue that both are interrelated activities and that the dichotomy is an illusion. The writing of fieldnotes includes "participating, observing and jotting notes" (p. 21). Emerson, Fretz and Shaw (2011) emphasize the importance of being aware of and noting insider terms and concepts as an essential part of taking fieldnotes.

In writing fieldnotes, the researcher engages various types of narrative and interpretive strategies. Often, it involves interpreting one type of activity or concept in terms of another. In this sense, fieldnotes also serve as the first step in the analysis of data. By trying to convey one set of concepts or cultural activity in more familiar terms, it allows readers to understand and get a little closer to the culture under study by making a connection to it. Another way of writing fieldnotes is to simply write down what happened during the day in chronological order. Such writing may seem episodic and disjointed without stories to connect one day or event with another, and yet the unfinishedness of such fieldnotes leaves analytical possibilities open. A third way to write fieldnotes is to combine the immediacy of writing as much as possible down along with engaging a reflective process periodically during fieldwork. To do this, one would write down the interactions, capture the insider terms as much as possible, write in chronological order, and then write periodic reflective notes on events, themes, and perhaps people or places. However comprehensive the fieldnotes might be, they always represent the eye of the researcher and the choices made during research. What to observe, what to pay attention to and what to relegate to the background while one focuses, and what ends up being written all represent the direction the researcher wishes to take. The researcher in the field writing notes is conspicuous and usually likes to avoid the actual writing while participating. Goffman (2014) and Venkatesh (2008) offer us some insights into how participants viewed their jottings in the field.

Goffman (2014) describes how the young Black men she ran the streets with, and in whose neighborhood she lived, viewed her. Being a White woman in a Black man's world, she was relegated to a safe role of "sister" or "godsister" to Mike, her main contact in the group. It was Mike who let it be known that he would not tolerate any advances towards his sister. In addition, Mike served as the main informant, who introduced Goffman as his "godsister" and opened doors for her, including guards of halfway houses whom she interviewed. In writing fieldnotes, Goffman describes that she wrote constantly and soon the young men, who hung around her apartment, would read over her shoulder and comment on or correct what she had written. She says that she wrote fieldnotes "most evenings and often throughout the morning and early afternoon as well" (Goffman, 2014, p. 435).

Writing fieldnotes while engaging in participant observation is difficult, a point acknowledged by Venkatesh (2008). It is also difficult to keep informing the participants that every word is being noted and, in fact, an ethnographer often wants participants to forget this fact and act normally. It is like a candid camera shot versus a posed one. Both are informative, but in different ways. At one point in the book, he describes his feelings after he casually mentioned to J.T., the leader of the Black Kings gang, that he had to go and "write some of this down." He immediately waited with bated breath wondering if J.T. would shut down his writing and access to the group, but to his relief, J.T. took his comment in stride. As Venkatesh acknowledged, "I had never actually told J.T. that I was keeping notes on all our conversations; I always waited until we split up before writing down what had transpired" (Venkatesh, 2008, p. 23). In the following exercise, try out a field observation and practice writing fieldnotes.

Try It Out: Research Journal Exercise 2.11

1. Choose a place to observe. You can try observing an activity for about 20 minutes. It is not necessary to know everyone you are observing. For this practice, you can choose a place where a lot of activity takes place. For example, you might want to observe the people interacting in a teacher's lounge at a school. Or you can watch how library spaces get used. Or what happens at a little league practice. Or you could just take a walk and observe what you see along the walk.

2. Decide how you will record the observation. Will you write while observing or after? What will you use to record—is

there going to be an element of audio or video or are you going to jot notes while observing?

3. What to observe?

   a. Look at the environment and write a description of where the action is taking place.
   b. If indoors, describe the walls, the decor, what is the place mainly used for? What is the neighborhood it is located in? What is the building like?
   c. If outdoors, describe the space and how and why people have gathered here, the neighborhood it is located in.
   d. Observe the interactions between people. What are they discussing? What are different people saying?
   e. What is the language they use that might be considered "insider language"?
   f. Describe the people.
   g. What is the main activity taking place?

4. Write in your journal how you made the decisions regarding what to observe.
5. What did you choose to focus on?
6. What was the main theme of what you wrote?
7. What are some challenges to writing fieldnotes that you observed in your exercise?
8. What was easy about writing fieldnotes?
9. How will you evaluate your fieldnotes?

Along with participant observation, interviews are the most commonly used tool for data gathering. In the next section we offer some suggestions and questions that will orient researchers to qualitative interviewing and the writing up of the interviews.

Writing Up Interviews

The standard suggestion for interviews is to tape and transcribe verbatim. It is a process that is usually implicitly taught, commonly by examples of fieldnotes. These allow students to process and learn for themselves what they should do with interview tapes and, as a result, questions that should be asked are swept under the carpet and rarely discussed. These questions include the rationale behind decisions to do with field note transcriptions, specifically interview transcripts.

Transcribing is not a mere mechanical act. It is in fact a rung in the ladder of data analysis. Scholars have pointed to the lack of attention given to transcriptions in qualitative research (Bird, 2005; Tilley, 2003). Transcripts are not presented as a series of choices made by the researcher and are instead presented as complete and transparent. Typically, transcription is approached either as a process that includes all the pauses, commas, and speech fillers (e.g., "er," "umm," "uh-huh," etc.) or in a way that eliminates all these pauses to give the effect of a whole text. The first approach might make it difficult for a reader since readers are not used to seeing all the pauses in print (Bucholtz, 2000). Transcriptions can also be regarded as the first stage of the analytical process (Hutchby and Wooffitt, 1998). Overall, it is important to exercise reflexivity in order to clarify and write up the transcription process (Bucholtz, 2007). Below, we offer an exercise that can assist researchers in thinking about the transcription process and its role in data analysis.

The following are adapted and extended from Devault (1990) and can be used as research journal exercises.

Try It Out: Research Journal Exercise 2.12

Questions to think about:

1. Should I record the interview?
2. What is a complete transcription?
3. What about editing? What is allowed and what is not allowed?
4. Am I allowed to excerpt from interviews and, if so, am I allowed to change anything?
5. What if participants want me to put into standard English the everyday slang that they used during the interview?

These questions are important since they remind the researcher to be attentive to the question of how to represent the words, thoughts, and "talk" of the participants. While it is standard practice in qualitative research for the researcher to edit the excerpts that they include in their published papers, it is less common to find any stated rationale for such decisions. Blauner (1987) explains that researchers engaged in life writing are more likely to be self-conscious about editing the voices of their participants. Editing includes changing or correcting grammar, vernacular English, and omitting pauses or awkward "umms" and "ahhs." One rationale for such omissions is to ensure that participants get a fair hearing. Researchers want the focus to be on what the participants said and worry that readers might form negative images of the participants because of non-standard grammar or particular turns of phrases. At times, such editing is done at the request of the participants. For example, Swaminathan (2004) in her work with immigrant women of the academy, found that some women whom she interviewed at times slipped into slang that they did not want reported in the finished writing product. Instead, they trusted her to edit their voices to sound polished and "literate." Editing to omit repetitions is another rationale for researchers to omit portions of participants' interviews. However, as Devault (1997) argues, such benign rationales tend to obscure the less than benign results of such editing. Women's words get distorted with such practices. In her research on women's practices of feeding the family, it was in those awkward pauses and hesitancies that she found analytic content that led her to understand the unacknowledged portions of women's work in the household. Paget (1981) further suggests that editing is a way by which emotions get suppressed. And emotions are often key indicators of what is happening and how events are affecting different participants.

Does this mean that all qualitative researchers should engage in the type of detailed conversational analysis that discourse analysts undertake? We would argue against such an approach and instead suggest that qualitative researchers undertake editing and detailed analyses strategically and mindfully. By asking oneself the questions above, it is possible to determine the extent to which editing is desirable.

If interview data are sent out to be transcribed, it is important to listen to the audio recording, compare the transcript, and fill in memories of the interview that are not necessarily audible. Such memories include body language or pauses or the general mood that you felt prevailed while the participant was relating the stories. What were the emotions that were associated with each story? Some questions to think about while comparing the audio recordings of interviews with transcripts are:

1) How is the audio different from the transcript?
2) Is speech quicker when we listen to it?
4) In the interview, are digressions pursued or ignored?
5) What is the tone? Relaxed, tense, or . . .?
6) What nuances of pauses, hesitancies, self-assurance or calmness of puzzlement can we glean from the voices?
7) What can we remember about the body language?

Try It Out: Research Journal Exercise 2.13

1. In your journal, write a short reflective note about the difference between reading a transcript and listening to an audio of an interview.
2. What did you add to your transcript after listening to the audio of the interview?

Data Analyses and the Process of Verification

In analyzing data, critical approaches would mean questioning not only what is apparent and evident but also to go beyond viewing data as impersonal and to look at the personal connections and meanings and emotions that data can sometimes evoke. Griffith and Smith (1987), in their study of how mothers organized their lives around the schooling process of their children, were struck by their own emotional responses to some processes of mothering. They compared the ways in which they had allowed their own children to watch TV while other mothers had taken children to Shakespearean plays. The point they make, however, is that such emotional responses on their part triggered their attention so that they began to notice the moral dimensions of mothering that are socially constructed and organized in society. Their own reactions were in part a response to the social script of mothering that incorporated a moral dimension. For researchers, therefore, it is important to question deeply their own responses and the origins of those responses. Some questions suggested below can serve as practice prompts to help identify and take note of emotions during the research process.

Try It Out: Research Journal Exercise 2.14

Questions that can guide us to move in this direction might include:

What am I feeling here? (identifying the response or emotion)
What is the source of this feeling?
What is my assumption regarding this act/thought?
What is the conflict I am experiencing?
Can I identify a norm in this context?

Data analysis remains a somewhat mysterious process and, after reading a study, we may still not quite understand some aspects of how the researcher carried out her study.

The following are questions to which readers of research often seek answers:

- What does the author mean by themes emerging from the data or the coding?
- How is triangulation arrived at?
- What is member checking?
- How did the data lead to further questioning and what were those follow-up questions?
- How is verification of data taking place if the term "triangulation" is not used?
- How is data trustworthiness determined?
- To what extent are participants part of the research process?

These are the same questions that a researcher can keep in mind when thinking through the process of verification and quality control in the research process.

Themes Emerging from Data

Qualitative researchers often describe their analyses of data in terms of themes emerging from data, leading one to conjecture whether there is a process inherent to raw data where one leaves it like bread dough to let it rise on its own and finds that it has magically reorganized itself into neat categories. Qualitative analyses mainly use inductive rather than deductive reasoning. Inductive processes rely on generating ideas from the data while deductive processes use data to confirm or negate a pre-formed idea. Qualitative research does not preclude the use of deductive analyses, although most texts describe the results of inductive analyses while leaving the process obscure. The process of analysis can be regarded as an explicit step in interpreting data as a whole, with specific strategies used to categorize and chunk data, or it can also be regarded as starting much earlier by including the decision-making that takes place all along the research process. Such decisions include thinking about methodological frameworks, strategies for data collection, and why and how the researcher regards some data as more relevant than others.

Strategies for Analysis

One strategy for analysis is the constant comparative method developed for grounded theory by Glaser and Strauss (1967). This involves taking one experience or one piece of data and looking across data sets to find similar experiences or data chunks. For example, this may involve looking at two interviews of first-year teachers and then further examining within those interviews their mentoring experiences. The constant comparative method would involve asking oneself the following analytical questions:

1. How is x's experience of mentoring similar to and different from y's experience?
2. Where were the mentors drawn for x and y?
3. Why are they different or similar?

In phenomenological research, we might look at the essence of experience rather than compare and contrast the different ways in which a phenomenon is experienced. In phenomenology, analytic questions might look like the following:

1. What is the experience of mentoring?
2. How do they describe mentoring as their lived experience?

In ethnographic analysis, the focus is on trying to understand the culture of a group within a context. Analysis involves looking at the ideas that emerge in the field as well as sorting and sifting through them to search for categories, look for inconsistencies or contradictions, and then generate conclusions regarding what is happening and why.

1. What are the shared events in this community?
2. What are accepted norms in this community?
3. Who is identified as an outsider?
4. What can be learned from the everyday interactions of people with each other?

In life writing, analysis involves examining the speech forms and patterns used by participants alongside the stories they tell. Through the stories that people tell, life writing also tells us how participants understand and make meaning of their lives. Questions in life writing analysis focus on the participants' storytelling.

1. What are the themes of the stories participants narrate?
2. How are the stories related to each other?
3. How do the participants understand, interpret, and describe their world?

Regardless of the type of qualitative pathway and how it is mapped, processes that we elaborate in Chapter 3 of this book, Morse (1994) reminds us that all qualitative analyses have some characteristics in common. They all involve comprehending the phenomenon under study and synthesizing the phenomenon so that the connections between different parts are clear. Theorizing involves thinking about why relations between sets of data or phenomena appear as they do and involves recontextualizing or presenting what is learned from the study in the context of how others have articulated the phenomenon. These questions provide the researcher with good clues as to methodological responsibility, which goes beyond mere procedural congruence or alignment (Kuntz, 2015). These are questions that the researcher needs to keep in mind as a tool for reflexivity as they embark on analysis and the writing up of their research.

Researchers often refer to "member checking" as a way to verify with participants the themes and patterns they were themselves discerning. However, such member checks may lead to a different type of understanding rather than a straightforward verification of what the researcher sees or does not see. For example, in a footnote, Lewis (2005) explains that there were competing narratives regarding the themes and patterns that she saw in the data, leading to a less than unanimous agreement among her participants regarding her data analyses.

Questions to Consider During the Process of Data Analysis

During data analysis, asking the following questions of one's data can stimulate different ways of looking at data and interpreting it.

Who: Who are the key figures in the setting? How do they interact with each other?

What: What activities do people engage in? What is obvious? What are the emotions of people that are on display and what undercurrents can be felt?

Where: Where do events take place? Are there different spaces for different types of conversations?

When: When do events occur? Is there a pattern to meetings and events? What events are considered important and why?

How: How do different people get what they want? How do they deal with conflict? How do they cope with challenges?

Why: Why is this data important?

Critical Friend Approach

The critical friend approach introduces yet another form and style of questioning that many qualitative researchers find helpful, some would say essential, to an in-depth, sophisticated data analysis as well as a shared co-production of the manuscript that results from the research project. While most of the literature related to "critical friend" concepts is rooted in discussions about K-12 environments (Moore and Carter-Hicks, 2014, p. 2.), there are core principles that are applicable to many forms of collaboration among professionals, including qualitative researchers.

The few studies that have examined the "critical friend" model within the context of higher education highlight the positive nature of receiving critical feedback in a supportive environment (Costantino, 2010) and delineating the structured protocol that is used to convey that feedback around a mutually agreed-upon central question or dilemma, such as the following:

1. Introduction
2. Presentation
3. Clarifying questions
4. Examination of work sample
5. Pause to reflect on warm and cool feedback
6. Warm and cool feedback (without the presenter)
7. Reflection by presenter
8. Debrief

(Moore and Carter-Hicks, 2014, p. 5)

This type of structured protocol used to guide a feedback process can be adapted readily for use between qualitative researchers who agree to serve as "critical friends" and can be organized around specific types of questions that can help facilitate the feedback exchange. Clarifying questions could be posed by the critical friend in order to ease the researcher into the layers of meaning that are available within the context of the study under examination. The different types of feedback (e.g., warm and cool feedback) refers to a spectrum of feedback that ranges from *warm* (supportive and focused on what is going well) to *cool* (unattached, using an analytical gaze, focusing on discernments) to *critical* (more challenging, skeptical, looking for possible redirection, highlighting potential structural flaws in the study).

A critical friends model, for qualitative researchers, can be adapted and further conceptualized as those who participate in reciprocal listening, sharing, and facilitating by way of using exploratory questions. Critical friends help each other maintain deep integrity by asking supportive questions that challenge assumptions, help the researcher re-examine their positionality throughout the research project, and gently refocus the researcher onto the next set of questions that may need to be asked to help align the data analysis with the RQs and the overall purpose of the study. At times a "critical friend" also serves as a steady co-writer who helps bring the manuscript into shape, refines the writing to reveal more nuanced understandings, continues to question and prompt the researcher to help deepen the analysis and the writing, and other responsibilities as negotiated among the co-authors. For a few examples of critical friend models in practice, see Alder and Mulvihill (2016), *The Show Choir Handbook*; Gale and Wyatt (2009), *Between the Two: A Nomadic Inquiry into Collaborative Writing and Subjectivity*; and Collier, Moffatt and Perry (2014), "Talking, Wrestling, and Recycling: An Investigation of Three Analytic Approaches to Qualitative Data in Education Research." Collier, Moffatt and Perry (2014) explicitly move through various questions for each theoretical perspective they encounter and make the results of their analysis very transparent as they engage reflexively with those questions.

Swaffield (2003) summarizes well the essence of critical friend models:

At the core of critical friendship is constructive, purposeful dialogue which is distinct from conversation or discussion. Critical Friend Group dialogue is characterized as being reciprocal, supportive, and cumulative [and is often] with the purpose of making practice[s] explicit, discussable, and transferrable.

Storey and Richard (2013) add:

> Thus, learning is central to critical friendship and relates to models of learning that emphasize constructivist and social approaches. The constant exchange of ideas and the search for shared meaning and common understanding is different from casual conversation or professional debate.

(p. 16)

The essential point here is that a critical friend can raise particular types of questions that researchers find valuable and these questions are often framed differently than the researcher themselves would generate. Critical friend models for qualitative research projects can range from a single exchange to an ongoing co-authorship relationship. The particular kind of reciprocal exchanges that are the bedrock of equitable co-authored projects accentuate the benefits of collaborative writing as a form of inquiry driven by the continual negotiation and renegotiation of the questions driving and surrounding the project.

Examples of questions critical friends might pose include:

1) In this research project, what was your preferred method for data analysis?
2) How did you generate themes or categories?
3) To what extent are these themes congruent with your initial questions?
4) What surprised you about these themes?
5) What made you angry?
6) What made you excited?
7) If another person was looking at what you wrote, how likely is it that they would draw different conclusions from the data?
8) In what ways is the research limited? What are its flaws?
9) Why should people care about the findings of your study?
10) What would you do differently, if you were to start your study over again?

Generating questions through a critical friends approach emphasizes an approach to questioning as a process of dialogue with the self and other that also allows for reflection on identity and positionality. In this chapter we have outlined the research process and the questions that may be used along the way to guide that process. In the next chapter, we outline some questions for specific approaches to qualitative research.

References

Agee, J. (2009). Developing qualitative research questions: A reflective process. *International Journal of Qualitative Studies in Education, 22*(4), 431–447.

Alder, A.L., & Mulvihill, T.M. (2016). *The show choir handbook*. Lanham, MD: Rowman & Littlefield.

Berg, B. (2008). *Qualitative research methods for the social sciences*. Boston, MA: Pearson.

Bernard, H.R. (2000). *Social research methods: Qualitative and quantitative methods*. Thousand Oaks, CA: Sage.

Bird, C.M. (2005). How I stopped dreading and learned to love transcription. *Qualitative Inquiry, 11*(2), 226–248.

Blauner, B. (1987). Problems of editing 'first-person' sociology. *Qualitative Sociology, 10*, 46–64.

Booth, A. (2006). Clear and present questions: Formulating questions for evidence based practice. (S. Cleyle) *Library Hi Tech, 24*(3), 355–368.

Booth, A. (2007). Blogs, wikis and podcasts: The 'evaluation bypass' in action? *Health Information and Libraries Journal, 24*(4), 298–302.

Bordage, G., & Dawson, B. (2003). Experimental study design and grant writing in eight steps and 28 questions. *Medical Education, 37*(4), 376–385.

Bucholtz, M. (2000). The politics of transcription. *Journal of Pragmatics, 32*(10), 1439–1465.

Bucholtz, M. (2007). Variation in transcription. *Discourse Studies, 9*(6), 784–808.

Charmaz, K. (2000). Grounded theory: Objectivist and constructivist methods. In N. Denzin & Y. Lincoln (Eds.), *Handbook of qualitative research* (2nd ed., pp. 509–535). Thousand Oaks, CA: Sage.

Charmaz, K. (2006). *Constructing grounded theory: A practical guide through qualitative research*. London: Sage.

Collier, D., Moffatt, L., & Perry, M. (2014). Talking, wrestling, and recycling: An investigation of three analytic approaches to qualitative data in education research. *Qualitative Research, 15*(3), 389–404.

Corbin, J., & Strauss, S. (2015). *Basics of qualitative research: Techniques and procedures for developing grounded theory*. Thousand Oaks, CA: Sage.

Costantino, T. (2010). The critical friends group: A strategy for developing intellectual community in doctoral education. *ie: Inquiry in Education, 1*(2), 5.

Creswell, J.W. (2007). *Qualitative inquiry and research design* (2nd ed.). Thousand Oaks, CA: Sage.

Crotty, M. (1998). *The foundations of social research: Meaning and perspective in the research process.* Thousand Oaks, CA: Sage.

Crumley, E., & Koufogiannakis, D. (2002). Developing evidence-based librarianship: Practical steps for implementation. *Health Information and Libraries Journal, 19*(2), 61–70.

Devault, M.L. (1990). Talking and listening from women's standpoint: Feminist strategies for interviewing and analysis. *Social Problems, 37*(1), 96–116. Retrieved from http://doi.org.proxy.bsu.edu/10.2307/800797

Devault, M.L. (1997). Personal issues in social research: Issues of production and interpretation. In R. Hertz (Ed.), *Reflexivity and voice* (pp. 216–228). Thousand Oaks, CA: Sage.

Eldredge, J.D. (2002). Evidence-based librarianship: What might we expect in the years ahead? *Health Information and Libraries Journal, 19*(2), 71–77.

Emerson, R.M., Fretz, R.I., & Shaw, L.L. (2011). *Writing ethnographic fieldnotes.* Chicago, IL: University of Chicago Press.

Flick, U. (2008). *Designing qualitative research.* London: Sage.

Fontana, A., & Frey, J. (2000). The interview: From structured questions to negotiated text. In N. Denzin & Y. Lincoln (Eds.), *Handbook of qualitative research* (pp. 645–672). Thousand Oaks, CA: Sage.

Gale, K., & Wyatt, J. (2009). *Between the two: A nomadic inquiry into collaborative writing and subjectivity.* Cambridge: Cambridge Scholars Publishing.

Glaser, B.G., & Strauss, A.L. (1967). *The discovery of grounded theory.* Hawthorne, NY: Aldine.

Glesne, C., & Peshkin, A. (1992). *Becoming qualitative researchers: An introduction.* White Plains, NY: Longman.

Goffman, A. (2014). *On the run: Fugitive life in an American city.* Chicago, IL: University of Chicago Press.

Griffith, A., & Smith, D.E. (1987). Constructing cultural knowledge: Mothering as discourse. In J. Gaskell & A. Mclaren (Eds.), *Women and education: A Canadian perspective* (pp. 87–104). Calgary, Alberta: Detselig.

Guba, E.G., & Lincoln, Y.S. (1989). *Fourth generation evaluation.* Newbury Park, CA: Sage.

Guba, E.G., & Lincoln, Y.S. (2005). Paradigmatic controversies, contradictions, and emerging confluences. In Norman K. Denzin and Yvonna S. Lincoln (Eds.), *The Sage handbook of qualitative research* (3rd ed., pp. 191–215). Thousand Oaks, CA: Sage.

Hutchby, I., & Wooffitt, R. (1998). *Conversation analysis: Principles, practices, and applications.* Malden, MA: Polity Press.

Janesick, V.J. (2000). The choreography of qualitative research design. In Denzin, N.K. & Lincoln, Y.S. (Eds.), *Handbook of qualitative research* (pp. 379–399). Thousand Oaks, CA: Sage Publications.

Kamberelis, G., & Dimitriadis, G. (2013). *Focus groups: From structured interviews to collective conversations.* New York, NY: Routledge.

Kuntz, A. (2015). *The responsible methodologist: Inquiry, truth-telling and social justice.* Walnut Creek, CA: Left Coast Press.

Lewis, A. (2005). *Race in the schoolyard: Negotiating the color line in classrooms and communities.* New Brunswick, NJ: Rutgers University Press.

Mantzoukas, Stefanos (2008). A review of evidence-based practice, nursing research and reflection: Levelling the hierarchy. *Journal of Clinical Nursing,* *17*(2), 214–223.

Mantzoukas, Stefanos, & Jasper, Melanie (2008). Types of nursing knowledge used to guide care of hospitalized patients. *Journal of Advanced Nursing,* *62*(3), 318–326.

Mason, J. (2002). *Qualitative researching.* London: Sage.

Maxwell, J.A. (2005). *Qualitative research design* (Vol. 41). Applied social research methods series. Thousand Oaks, CA: Sage.

Mendelsohn, D.J. (1984). There are strategies for listening. *TEAL Occasional Papers,* *8,* 63–76.

Merriam, S.B. (1998). *Qualitative research and case study applications in education: Revised and expanded from case study research in education.* San Francisco, CA: Jossey-Bass Publishers.

Metz, M.H. (2001). Intellectual border crossing in graduate education: A report from the field. *Educational Researcher,* *30*(5), 1–7.

Miles, M.B., & Huberman, A.M. (1994). *Qualitative data analysis: An expanded sourcebook.* Thousand Oaks, CA: Sage.

Mishler, E.G. (1986). *Research Interviewing: Context and narrative.* Cambridge, MA: Harvard University Press.

Moore, J.A., & Carter-Hicks, J. (2014). Let's talk! Facilitating a faculty learning community using a critical friends group approach. *International Journal for the Scholarship of Teaching and Learning,* *8*(2), 9.

Morse, J.M. (1994). *Critical issues in Qualitative research methods.* Thousand Oaks, CA: Sage.

Morse, J.M., & Richards, L. (2002). *Read me first for a user's guide to qualitative research.* Thousand Oaks, CA: Sage.

Mueller, T.G., & Buckley, P.C. (2014). The odd man out: How fathers navigate the special education system. *Remedial and Special Education,* *35*(1), 40–49.

Okley, J., & Callaway, H. (1992). *Anthropology and autobiography.* London: Routledge.

Osada, N. (2004). Listening comprehension research: A brief review of the past thirty years. *Dialogue,* *3,* 53–66.

Oxford, R.L. (1993). Research update on teaching listening. *System, 21,* 205–211.

Pack, S. (2006). How they see me vs. how I see them: The ethnographic self and the personal self. *Anthropological Quarterly, 79*(1), 105–122.

Paget, M.A. (1981). The ontological anguish of women artists. *The New England Sociologist, 3,* 65–79.

Patton, M.Q. (2002). *Qualitative research and evaluation methods.* Thousand Oaks, CA: Sage.

Petticrew, M., & Roberts, H. (2008, April 15). *Systematic reviews in the social sciences: A practical guide.* New York, NY: John Wiley & Sons.

Price, B. (2002). Laddered questions and qualitative data research interviews. *Journal of Advanced Nursing, 37*(3), 273–281.

Qureshi, R. (2010). Ethical standards and ethical environment: Tension and a way forward. In F. Shamim & R. Qureshi (Eds.), *Perils, pitfalls and reflexivity in qualitative research in education* (pp. 78–100). London: Oxford University Press.

Radway, J. (1984). *Reading the romance: Women, patriarchy and popular culture.* Chapel Hill, NC: University of North Carolina Press.

Richardson, W., & Wilson, M.C. (1997). On questions, background and foreground. *Evidence Based Healthcare Newsletter, 17,* 8–9.

Riessman, C.K. (1987). When gender is not enough: Women interviewing women. *Gender and Society, 1*(2), 172–207.

Schardt, C., Adams, M.B., Owens, T., Keitz, S., & Fontelo, P. (2007). Utilization of the PICO framework to improve searching PubMed for clinical questions. *BMC Medical Informatics and Decision Making, 7*(1), 16.

Schwandt, T.A. (1996). Farewell to criteriology. *Qualitative Inquiry, 2,* 58–72.

Simmons, R. (2002). *Odd girl out: The hidden culture of aggression in girls.* Orlando, FL: Harcourt Press.

Smith, D. (1987). *The everyday world as problematic: A feminist sociology.* Boston, MA: Northeastern University Press.

Spender, D. (1980). *Man made language.* London: Routledge.

Spradely, J. (1979). *The ethnographic interview.* Belmont, CA: Cengage.

Stanko, E. (1985). *Intimate intrusions: Women's experience of male violence.* Boston, MA: Routledge.

Storey, V.A., & Richard, B. (2013). Carnegie project for the educational doctorate: The role of critical friends in diffusing doctoral program innovation. In C.A. Mullen & K.E. Lane (Eds.), *Becoming a global voice the 2013 yearbook of the National Council of Professors of Educational Administration.* Ypsilanti, MI: NCPEA Publications. Retrieved June 30, 2016, from https://www.researchgate.net/publication/240917871_Carnegie_Project_for_the_Educational_Doctorate_The_role_of_critical_friends_in_diffusing_doctoral_program_innovation

Strauss, A., & Corbin, J. (1998). *Basics of qualitative research: Techniques and procedures for developing grounded theory.* Thousand Oaks, CA: Sage.

Swaffield, S. (2003, January). The local education adviser as critical friend: Superman/woman or mission impossible? *Paper presented at Leadership for Learning: the Cambridge Network, 16th International Congress for School Effectiveness and Improvement, Sydney, January 5–8.* Retrieved December 11, 2016, from www.edu.cam.ac.uk

Swaminathan, R. (2004). Relational worlds: South Asian immigrant women talk about home/work. In M. Alfred & R. Swaminathan (Eds.), *Immigrant women of the academy: Negotiating boundaries, crossing borders in higher education* (pp. 89–104). New York, NY: Nova Science Press.

Tilley, S.A. (2003). "Challenging" research practices: Turning a critical lens on the work of transcription. *Qualitative Inquiry, 9*(5), 750–773.

Tracy, S.J. (2010). Qualitative quality: Eight "big-tent" criteria for excellent qualitative research. *Qualitative Inquiry, 16*(10), 837–851.

Venkatesh, S. (2008). *Gang leader for a day.* New York, NY: Penguin Press.

Werdmann, A.M., & King, J. (1984). Teaching teachers to question questions. *Literacy Research and Instruction, 23*(3), 218–225.

Wilen, W., & Clegg, A. (1986). Effective questions and questioning: A research review. *Theory and Research in Social Education, XIV*(2), 153–161.

Yin, R.K. (1994). *Case study research: Design and methods.* Beverly Hills, CA: Sage.

Yin, R.K. (2011). *Qualitative research from start to finish.* New York, NY: Guilford Publications.

3

MAPPING DIVERSE PATHWAYS

Chapter Summary

This chapter will discuss different approaches to qualitative research and draw on examples from studies to illustrate the differences between the types of questions within each approach. The chapter addresses the alignment between questions and each approach and how questions operate differently through the lifecycle of the project.

1. Questions for a phenomenological study
2. Questions for an ethnographic study
3. Questions for life writing approaches
4. Questions for a feminist study
5. Questions for participatory action research studies

Questions ought to help qualitative researchers map diverse pathways to knowledge. These pathways are shaped by epistemologies. Epistemologies are various ways that we understand the nature of knowledge and this is important to know for qualitative researchers because it helps determine the manner in which we will proceed to gather, analyze, and represent data. Furthermore it shapes the type of questions that are deemed answerable and the accompanying methods or procedures that appropriately align with a given epistemology.

The following might help to exemplify this alignment process between methodological approach and the types of questions that can be generated.

> **Subject (i.e., a broad-based starting point or topic under consideration):** Person and apple
>
> **Question 1 (Phenomenology):** How does the person experience the phenomenon of growing, preparing, and/or eating an apple?
>
> **Question 2 (Ethnography):** What is the surrounding culture/sub-culture that pre-disposes understandings about the relationship between the person and an apple? What would insider and outsider perspectives reveal?
>
> **Question 3 (Life writing):** What primary and secondary documents exist that would provide insights into the role apples played in the life of an individual? What stories do they tell about apples? What photographs do they have where apples are included?
>
> **Question 4 (Feminist):** What evidence do we have regarding who grows apples and who prepares it as food/decor? Who owns the orchards where the apple was grown? Is such ownership and consumerism linked to power issues? Do these power issues reflect traditional gender roles or do they deconstruct such roles?
>
> **Question 5 (Participatory action research):** What do the people (the growers, buyers, consumers) think are the main issues that need investigating? How can we negotiate with the stakeholders to figure out the problems that need further examination?

Exercises such as this can quickly be generated by researchers to help map the various types of questions linked to any qualitative research project. From these questions, a study can take further shape, allowing the questions to drive the methodological design and the methods that move the action steps forward when doing the research.

Mapping Approaches to Qualitative Research

In an article that analyzed middle school science students and their skills in asking critical questions, Cuccio-Schirripa and Steiner suggested that "questioning is one of the thinking processing skills which is structurally embedded in the thinking operation of critical thinking, creative thinking, and problem solving" (Cuccio-Schirripa and Steiner, 2000, p. 210). Questioning is a learned skill and, in qualitative research, one of the key points of approaching research critically is to engage in questioning oneself and one's prior assumptions in addition to questioning and reflecting on the different decisions you need to make as a researcher embarking on a journey. In Chapter 2, we explained and discussed questions that can be asked along the research journey and the differences between 1) research questions; 2) questions for fieldwork, interview questions, and analyses; and 3) questions for writing. In this chapter, we now want to dig deeper to get at the differences between the broad types of qualitative research and the alignment of the research questions with the decision-making processes of gathering/collecting data and analyzing data. If you are engaged in an ethnography, feminist study, or life writing project, what types of data would you gather and what questions can guide you based on the particular type of study you selected?

Questions for a Phenomenological Study

Cohen, M.Z. & Omery, A. (1994) has pointed out that phenomenological study is "tough stuff, very abstract and very conceptual" (p. 134). Despite increasing numbers of articles and published works as well as methods books on phenomenological research, there appears to be some degree of difficulty related to starting a phenomenological study, especially for those new to qualitative research. There is a lack of clarity regarding method and methodology where phenomenology is concerned. While methodology is distinguished from method, with the former being regarded as an approach and a philosophical grounding, the latter comprises techniques and procedures. The two challenges that researchers often face are: 1) understanding the philosophical underpinnings of phenomenology, and 2) having some clarity on the procedural aspects of carrying out a phenomenological research study.

Some structural elements of qualitative studies and in particular of phenomenological studies described by scholars are those of context description (Giorgi, 1997, 2005) and "deliberate naiveté" (Kvale and Brinkmann, 2009). Giorgi (1997, 2005) provided some ideas about phenomenological interviewing that differ from general qualitative interviewing. In his view, phenomenological interviews need to have a two-tiered approach. The first tier of questions would be focused on obtaining descriptions of context and the second tier of questions would elicit meaning. However, Giorgi (1997) offered no advice regarding how a phenomenological interview should proceed other than offering the generalist qualitative interview advice to keep questions broad and open ended. Kvale and Brinkmann (2009) regarded qualitative interviewing as a craft and built into their interviewing structure "deliberate naiveté." They also advised that phenomenological qualitative questions should aim to describe specific situations and actions and not general opinions. Seidman (2006) offered further ideas and suggestions regarding phenomenological interviewing. According to Seidman, three interviews per person were necessary. The first interview would focus on a life history that provided context, followed by an interview aimed to reconstruct the experience being investigated, and finally a third interview based on reflection where the participant would be able to reflect on the meaning of the experience. Seidman recommended that interview questions be open ended and be built from the context of the first interview and that interview guides or protocols be used with caution and flexibility.

For the interviewer to undertake phenomenological interviewing, it is important that there is phenomenological reduction on the part of the researcher. This is done by becoming a perpetual beginner (Merleau-Ponty, 1962) or through "bracketing" (Husserl, 1970), which means setting aside what one already knows about a given phenomenon. Total abstention is acknowledged as impossible to achieve and therefore "bracketing" is used as a way for the researcher to become aware of her assumptions and as a means to overcome the taken-for-granted views of the natural attitude. This process is more akin to a dialogue with the self—a reflexivity exercise that allows one to ask questions of oneself and, when posing interview questions to the participant, the researcher then is self-conscious of their own assumptions. The phenomenological reduction is a process by which the researcher commits to an attitudinal shift or the epoche. Epoche is a critical stance adopted by the researcher whereby the researcher resolves to take nothing for granted.

Although phenomenological research is considered to be interpretive rather than critical qualitative research, it is nevertheless true that often, as a result of phenomenological research, change can occur as a result of awareness on the part of participants. While that may or may not be part of the agenda of the researcher, it is also important for researchers to be aware that, regardless of the type of research they undertake, there is a possibility that change might occur.

Features of Phenomenological Studies

Main objective: Understanding the essence of experience (Crotty, 1998), including lived experiences such as lived space, lived time, lived body (Van Manen and Adams, 2010). Lived space grounds a person in their location. Van Manen called this "felt space" and said that the space in which we are located affects us. Impersonal spaces affect us as much as spaces where we feel at home.

Live time: subjective time as opposed to objective clock time (Van Manen, 1990).

Live body: Concept of embodiment that we are always in our body (Van Manen, 1990). Body language is an example of what we reveal or conceal from another. Lived human relation is the lived relation we maintain with others in the interpersonal space we share with them (Van Manen, 1990).

Philosophers and scholars associated with phenomenology: Gadamer (2004), Giorgi (1997, 2005), Merleau-Ponty (1962/1995), Moustakas (1994), Van Manen (1990).

Main types of phenomenology: Descriptive, interpretive

- Describing the general characteristics of a phenomenon rather than an individual's experiences (Giorgi, 2008).
- Phenomenological reduction or bracketing or epoche is the distinguishing feature of phenomenology—the suspension of the researcher's beliefs, prejudices, and preconceptions,

as well as getting back to the pre-reflective state to describe the phenomenon in its purest form as it occurred.

- When researchers adopt a phenomenological attitude, they are open to a sense of wonder and curiosity while engaging in reflexivity (Finlay, 2009).

Ethnography: In ethnographic studies, the aim is to understand cultural patterns and shared human experiences within a particular self-defined group or a group as perceived by outsiders. The aims may be also directed towards solving a particular problem. For example, an ethnographic study was commissioned by a school to better understand the experiences of teachers in a new bi-lingual program adopted by the school.

Characteristics of ethnography: Fieldwork or time spent on site in research is a key characteristic of ethnography.

Primary research tool: Participant observation is the main tool for ethnographers and involves a continuous reflexive engagement both with participants and with oneself. The distinction between what participants do and what they say they do is often emphasized. This mode of research has been challenged for centralizing the role of the researcher rather than those of participants and, consequently, there has been a move to shift from "participant observation to the observation of participation" (Tedlock, 1991).

Writing in ethnography: Fieldnotes are first written followed by analytic memos to oneself to link the different themes one sees in the field (Emerson, 2011).

Collaborative ethnography: Research in ethnography has moved away from the single researcher authorship to a more collaborative style reminiscent of life writing. In recent years, collaborative ethnographies acknowledge the presence and role of key informants (see for example, Elyachar, 2005; Narayan, 1997).

Writing of ethnographies: Detailed ethnographic accounts with extended direct quotes and fieldnotes are typical of ethnographic writing.

Focused ethnography: While one of the key features of an ethnographic study is to spend long hours in the field (Wolcott, 2001), there is a compressed research design in ethnography that is also used by student researchers. This is referred to as focused ethnography. In focused ethnography, the time period may vary and be as short as three days or as long as six to eight weeks. Data are gathered through focus groups, participant observation methods, and interviews with key participants with the goal of understanding a single cultural domain or event in order to either learn from the event for an appropriate intervention or for creating change.

What is Life Writing Research?

Life writing is an umbrella term that comprises a variety of methods and approaches. The most popular approaches within life writing are autobiography, biography, autoethnography, oral history, and life history (Mulvihill and Swaminathan, 2017). Research within life writing can take any of the above forms. While each approach is different, there are commonalities that tie them together. The aim of life writing is ultimately to understand and open up a life so that, through the story of one life, we can understand the human experience. Some features of life writing include:

- Valuing the experiences of participants
- Valuing the personal details
- Valuing context
- Valuing the relationship between the life writer and the narrator or participant
- Valuing sharing and communicating knowledge and stories of lives

A few questions that life writers can put to themselves when beginning engaging with life writing methods are:

1. Why would a reader be interested in this life? This prompts the "so what" question that is integral to all research. It allows the researcher to think through the choice of subject and topic in life writing. Why this person or this group of people?
2. What sources of data will I use to research this life?
3. What is the relationship between the life writer and the narrator?

Life writers use a variety of sources ranging from interviews that rely on memories to archival data to letters, journals, photographs, and conversations with the narrator and with others who were acquainted with the narrator/subject. The relationship between the life writer and the narrator is more equitable in some forms of life writing (e.g., life history) than in other forms (e.g., biography). Life writers depend on memory as a data source for making meaning. However, memory is contextual and the politics of remembering remind us to question what is remembered or forgotten. DeSalvo's (1998) advice to "aspiring educational biographers" stands true for all life writing researchers. She urges that researchers take a stance that allows them to empathize with the narrator or subject of their work and not stand apart, in judgment. She points out that the work of biography involves the engagement of emotions and intellect on the part of the biographer or life writer who also needs to challenge any lingering fear and discomfort in the effort to chart a full picture of the life of their subject.

The following questions can guide the life writer who is working with stories and lives:

1. Whose story am I interested in?
2. Who is telling the story?
3. Who owns this story?
4. What is the best way to re-tell this story?
5. Who gets represented in the story?

DeSalvo (1998), on a lighthearted note, also asks aspiring biographers to try to keep a balance between their own lives and their work so that the work does not engulf their lives to a point where every conversation begins with a new anecdote about a discovery in the archives. In the following exercise, you can hold an imaginary dialogue with your participant or subject to understand and go beyond the narrative.

Try It Out: Research Journal Exercise 3.1

1. Find a story told to you by the participant or one that you found compelling in the documents, diaries, and other notes that you are using as data.

2. Rewrite the story in about 250–300 words.
3. Ask questions that come to your mind about the story.
4. What would you like to know or ask the participant that will illuminate the context of the story?
5. Whose story is this and why was it important to you?
6. What criteria did you use to choose this story to analyze or re-tell?
7. Reflect on your own position in this story.

In the next section, we tackle a third approach—that of a feminist perspective to questions in qualitative research.

What is a Feminist Research Perspective?

Feminist research advocates a commitment to openness, description, and understanding. Feminist research investigates the everyday, the personal, the lived experiences of women (Stanley and Wise, 1993). Feminists seek to overturn or critique the positivistic framework of research so that women's lives and experiences would not be misconstrued and would instead emerge from concealment.

According to Bartky, becoming a feminist involved a personal transformation in consciousness or what feminists refer to as "consciousness raising."

A feminist project has the following characteristics:

• Research done by, for, and about women
• Women and gender as the focus of analysis
• Importance of consciousness raising
• Rejection of the concept of participant as subject
• Reduction of the distance between participant and researcher
• Collaborative research effort between researcher and participant
• Goal of empowerment and emancipation
• Concern with ethics

Relationship between the Researcher and the Researched

Feminist approaches utilize "friendship" as a type of collaboration that requires "radical reciprocity" that moves from "studying them to studying us" (Tillmann-Healy, 2003, p. 735).

There is a mutuality or mutual exchange in this relationship. They also consider the research process as a dialogue between the participant and the researcher. "Both are assumed to be individuals who reflect upon their experience and who can communicate those reflections" (Acker, Barry and Esseveld, 1983, p. 427). Participatory action research studies and feminist approaches seek out participant voices in a variety of ways.

Participatory Action Research

Participatory action research (PAR) is a research process where both participation and action are highlighted in the research process. The goal of the research is to collaborate with participants on an issue or problem with the ultimate objective of finding a solution together that can be implemented. The process is cyclical and identifying and agreeing on the issue is followed by planning strategies leading to action to gather data and analyze the data. Following this is the implementation process and evaluation or examining the issue again to find new issues. PAR represents a relation that is continuous and long term, with the benefits of research immediately applicable to the problems raised by participants. Park (1997) referred to PAR as "research of the people, by the people and for the people" (p. 8), and Kemmis and McTaggart (2005) have pointed out that PAR is research with and not on a group of people.

The degree to which participants and researchers collaborate is central to PAR. While one end of the continuum has participants or the community taking charge of the research enterprise, at the other end, we have researchers positioning the participants as consultants or as token representatives with no real power to participate or get involved. The participation continuum or the varying degrees of collaboration is best described by Cornwall (1996). She describes the following roles that the participants and researchers can adopt that can lead to varying degrees of collaboration:

a) Participants have no power but representatives are chosen to be part of the research. Cornwall refers to this as "co-option."

b) Participants do not make decisions regarding priorities but are assigned tasks. Cornwall refers to this as "compliance."

c) Participants are asked to give their opinions but do not have decision-making power. Cornwall refers to this form of participation as "consultation."

d) Participants and researchers or those outside the community work together but the direction is still decided by the researchers. This form of participation is "cooperation."

e) Participants and researchers share information and knowledge based on which both agree on strategies and plan together. This is referred to as "co-learning."

f) Participants decide the agenda and make plans without any intervention from researchers. This is referred to as "collective action" by Cornwall.

Cornwall's (1996) continuum points to the variability present in PAR. The most desirable of these roles for researchers is to find a "co-learning" context. Equality of status between the researchers and participants is one of the goals of PAR. However, it is also true that participation need not be "fixed" in PAR into any of these categories since participants' roles are likely to change over the course of the research. They may participate more in the planning or implementation phases and less in the writing up of the research phase. One set of questions to pose to both oneself as a researcher and to the participants is to determine how much participation is possible and what is meaningful participation from the point of view of participants. The following questions can serve as a reminder:

1. Is the purpose of the project clear to all parties?
2. Who benefits from this project?
3. What counts as participation, given any constraints that participants might face in their contexts?
4. How are participants chosen?

One of the features of PAR that other qualitative research methods share to some degree is the core necessity to build trusting relationships with participants. Since collaborative research is essential to PAR, it is important for researchers to spend time in the setting. The other feature of PAR that makes it unsettling to many researchers is the fluid design of PAR. Since priorities and agendas are set together with participants in the desired co-learning model, it means that research design cannot be fully set before the start of the research. While this is true for almost all qualitative research, the difference in PAR is that the direction of the research is also determined at least partially by the participants' wishes.

In Tables 3.1 and 3.2, a summary of the research approaches, research goals, the role of the researcher, and the different research questions for each approach are outlined.

TABLE 3.1 Summary of Approaches, Goals, Data, and Researcher role

Approaches to QR	Goal	Data Gathering	Relationship of Researcher–Participant
Phenome-nology	Understand and convey the essence of the phenomenon	Interviews	Researcher often has experience of the phenomenon under consideration and needs to "bracket" or set aside preconceived ideas based on personal experiences
Ethnography	Understand what makes up the culture of a group of people, place, or activity; use cultural concepts to guide research; explain and interpret data	Use of open-ended interviews; participant observation; informal conversations; participation/ observation of key events, rituals, ceremonies	Researcher relationship develops and deepens over time; reflexivity should be aimed at trying to learn the culture from the perspective of participants

Approaches to QR	Goal	Data Gathering	Relationship of Researcher–Participant
Life writing	Understand key events, relationships in the life of a person	Interviews, documents, archives	Researcher relationship deepens over time and as the researcher learns more about the participant/ subject; reflexivity and imagination are needed to fill in the gaps left by limited sources
Feminist	Understand women's perspectives and experiences with a view to empowerment, affirmation, consciousness raising	Collaborative interviewing	Collaborative relationship; the goal is to make the researcher– participant relationship as equal as possible
Participatory action research	Empowerment of the community and participants	Collaborative agenda, question generation, planning, thinking, acting, and implementing	Collaborative relationship; the participants participate in most aspects of the research and offer input during all stages of the research/ action

Different approaches to qualitative research generate a variety of questions and allow the researcher to think about the diverse ways in which research can be conducted. In order to think about which approach would be most appropriate, the following questions can serve as a catalyst.

TABLE 3.2 Examples of Research Questions for Each Approach

Approaches	Research Questions Examples	Questions for Each Approach
Phenomenology	What are first-year teachers' experiences of school? How do men/women make meaning of caregiving?	How do x experience y? What are x's experiences of y? How do x make meaning of y?
Ethnography	How do federal abstinence-only education policies shape students' experiences of sex and sexuality in high schools?	What is the culture of a group of people? How is a culture created and sustained? What types of rituals, meetings, and events sustain culture? What types of actions nurture a particular culture?
Life writing	How did Montessori's own life experiences influence her philosophy and method of instruction?	What are the significant events in the life of Montessori that can cast some light on how she developed her philosophy of teaching?
Feminist	What are the experiences of rural women who move to cities to work in India?	How do the experiences of women relate to the structure and power relations in society? How do women feel empowered?
Participatory action research	How can a community develop projects for alternative local food sources?	How do community members and researchers collaborate to create urban organic gardens?

Try It Out: Research Journal Exercise 3.2

• Take your research question and write it up as if the study was a phenomenological study.

- Now rewrite the question to make it an ethnographic study.
- Rewrite the question to make it a feminist-focused study or a participatory action research study or a life writing study.
- What is different about each type of study question?
- What changes in each approach?
- What is the role of the researcher in each approach?
- What is the role of the participant in each approach?

Writing qualitative research can be a fun, invigorating time and, at the same time, can also lead one to moments of despair as one sits down to write surrounded by vast amounts of data piles that stare back at one defiantly. At such moments, the following questions can serve as a reminder or prompt to focus on the narrative or story.

Questions to Consider When Creating Narratives from Interview Transcripts

What is the story or narrative that stands out?

What portions of the interview transcripts or fieldnotes feel most exciting to me?

Why am I interested in this particular story?

Is there a story here that I am missing?

How would another researcher approach this data?

If I were to give a 30 minute talk about my data, what parts would I highlight?

In this chapter we have outlined what questions can guide a researcher through several approaches in qualitative research. In writing the narrative, the researcher has to make choices regarding what story to tell and whose story to highlight and how to narrate it so that the story conveys the meanings that the researcher and narrator intend. Reflexivity tools, as outlined in the next chapter, can assist the researcher in this regard.

References

Acker, J., Barry, K., & Esseveld, J. (1983, December). Objectivity and truth: Problems in doing feminist research. *Women's Studies International Forum, 6*(4), 423–435.

Cohen, M.Z. & Omery, A. (1994). Dialogue: Clarifying phenomenological methods. In J. Morse (Ed.), *Critical issues in qualitative research methods* (pp. 134–136). Thousand Oaks, CA: Sage.

Crotty, M. (1998). *The foundations of social research: Meaning and perspective in the research process.* Thousand Oaks, CA: Sage.

Cuccio-Schirripa, S., & Steiner, H.E. (2000). Enhancement and analysis of science question level for middle school students. *Journal of Research in Science Teaching, 37*, 210–224.

DeSalvo, L. (1998). Advice to aspiring educational biographers. In C. Kridel (Ed.), *Writing educational biography* (pp. 269–271). New York, NY: Routledge.

Elyachar, Julia. (2005). *Markets of dispossession: NGOs, economic development, and the state in Cairo.* Durham, NC: Duke University Press.

Emerson, R.M., Fretz, R.I., & Shaw, L.L. (2011). *Writing ethnographic fieldnotes.* Chicago, IL: University of Chicago Press.

Finlay, L. (2009). Debating phenomenological research methods. *Phenomenology and Practice, 3*(1), 6–25.

Gadamer, H.G. (2004). *Truth and method* (2nd ed.). London: Sheed and Ward Stagbooks.

Giorgi, A. (1997). The theory, practice and evaluation of the phenomenological method as a qualitative research procedure. *Journal of Phenomenological Psychology, 28*, 235–260.

Giorgi, A. (2005). The phenomenological movement and research in the human sciences. *Nursing Science Quarterly, 18*(1), 75–82.

Giorgi, A. (2008). Concerning a serious misunderstanding of the essence of the phenomenological method in psychology. *Journal of Phenomenological Psychology, 39*, 33–58.

Husserl, E. (1970). *The crisis of European sciences and transcendental phenomenology: An introduction to phenomenological philosophy* (D. Carr, Trans.). Evanston, IL: Northwestern University Press.

Kemmis, S., & McTaggart, R. (2005). Participatory action research: Communicative action and the public sphere. In N.K. Denzin & Y.S. Lincoln (Eds.), *The Sage handbook of qualitative research* (3rd ed., pp. 559–603). London: Sage.

Kvale, S., & Brinkmann, S. (2009). *Interviews: Learning the craft of qualitative research interviewing.* Thousand Oaks, CA: Sage.

Merleau-Ponty, M. (1962/1995). *Phenomenology of perception.* (Colin Smith, Trans.). New York, NY: Routledge.

Moustakas, C. (1994). *Phenomenological research methods.* Thousand Oaks, CA: Sage.

Mulvihill, T., & Swaminathan, R. (2017). *Critical approaches to life writing in qualitative research.* New York, NY: Routledge.

Narayan, K. In collaboration with Sood, U.D. (1997). *Mondays on the dark night of the moon: Himalayan foothill folktales.* New York, NY: Oxford University Press.

Park, P. (1997). Participatory research, democracy, and community. *Practicing Anthropology, 19*(3), 8–13.

Seidman, I.E. (2006). *Interviewing as qualitative research: A guide to researcher in education and the social sciences* (3rd ed.). New York: Teachers College Press.

Stanley, L., & Wise, S. (1993). *Breaking out again: Feminist epistemology and ontology.* New York, NY: Routledge.

Tedlock, B. (1991). From participant observation to the observation of participation: The emergence of narrative ethnography. *Journal of Anthropological Research, 47*(1), 69–94.

Tillmann-Healy, Lisa M. (2003). Friendship as method. *Qualitative Inquiry, 9*(5), 729–749.

Van Manen, M. (1990). *Researching lived experience: Human science for an action sensitive pedagogy.* London, Ontario: Althouse Press.

Van Manen, M., & Adams, C.A. (2010). Phenomenology. In Penelope Peterson, Eva Baker, & Barry McGaw (Eds.), *International encyclopedia of education* (Vol. 6, pp. 449–455). Oxford: Elsevier.

Wolcott, H.F. (2001). *Writing up qualitative research.* Thousand Oaks, CA: Sage.

4

CRITICAL REFLEXIVITY AND ARTFUL QUESTIONING

This chapter explores various ways critical reflexivity can be fostered and how "artful" questioning can help the researcher reflect on the research process through the journey from start to finish. Investigating the assumptions we hold as researchers provides opportunities to develop artful questions aimed at deepening our ability to understand and make transparent our positionality. This chapter will offer ways to create critical reflexivity questions for all dimensions of the study.

Asking questions is integral to the process of reflexivity. In all stages of the research process, questions that are approached critically can enhance and serve as tools that can stimulate deeper work, creative thinking, and a more complex analysis.

Defining Reflexivity

Qualitative researchers accept that reflexivity is an essential component of the process; however, the ways in which reflexivity in the research process is defined and understood are varied. What is reflexivity and what is the difference between reflection and reflexivity? Reflection is a term often found in the qualitative research methodological literature, and at times seems to be conflated with the term reflexivity. Yet for our purposes we hold these terms as companion terms with distinctions, whereby reflection is a subset or part of the larger, more broadly encompassing activities that fall under the term reflexivity. Reflexivity is a term that has been examined by several scholars and has been variously defined or described as a process that demands that "we interrogate ourselves concerning the ways in which research is shaped and staged around the contradictions and paradoxes of our own lives" (Lincoln and Guba, 2003, p. 283).

To be reflexive, a researcher has an ongoing internal conversation that asks two questions—first, what does the researcher know and second, how does the researcher know it? Reflexivity implies learning to pay attention to the social context in which the researcher is embedded. It means being aware of habits of thought that are a product of one's place in the social structure. Reflexivity, or the process by which the gaze of the researcher is turned upon oneself, has a long history in the field of qualitative research. Often regarded as "confessional tales" (Sparkes, 2002; Van Maanen, 2011), accounts included researchers' dilemmas, tensions, decision-making efforts, and issues that came up during the research. These "confessional tales" were usually published parallel with rather than integrated into the objective "realist" tales that focused solely on the participants rather than the interaction between the participant and the researcher. In realist tales, the voice of the researcher was minimized. Over time, scholars have advocated for an integration of the realist and the confessional tale (Sparkes, 2002) or publication alongside each other without replacing any one of the accounts with the other.

Hesse-Biber and Leavy emphasize the reflexivity process as perspective-taking even before the research begins in the field. The process begins with a critical look at one's own values and how our environment or social positioning has influenced the ways in which we think. The purpose of this examination is to get an understanding of how our thinking processes and attitudes can influence our research. In their words:

> The reflexive researcher's perspective begins with an understanding of the importance of one's own values and attitudes in relation to the research process. This recognition begins prior to

entering the field. Reflexivity means taking a critical look inward and reflecting on one's lived reality and experiences; this self-reflection or journey can be extremely helpful in the research process. Reflexivity is the process through which a researcher recognizes, examines, and understands how his or her social background and assumptions can intervene in the research process.

(Hesse-Biber and Leavy, 2007, pp. 129–130)

The purpose of engaging in reflexivity throughout the research process is to intentionally raise questions that help sharpen the analysis. It can emerge from either a desire to challenge the status quo power relations in the research process and/or it can be a form of strengthening the overall trustworthiness of the study. The latter practices of attempting to affirm data as "truth" has been critiqued as a post-positivist ideal and has since given way to a radical reflexivity where the researcher learns to embrace the socially constructed nature of the research experience. Taylor (1995) suggests that reflexivity may be a radical action when it is understood as an awareness of being self-aware. In his words, "when I examine my own experience, or scrutinize my own thinking, reflexivity takes a radical turn" (p. 57). In this sense, Taylor is referring to a reflexivity that is the product of a dialogue with the self. Reflexivity and questions to stimulate reflexive processes can mean paying attention to one's own emotions during the research process. What appears disturbing or what makes one curious are clues to our assumptions and levels of comfort or discomfort with what we see or hear. Leary, Minichiello and Kottler (2009) describe their emotional responses to participants in their study. They share their frustrations, overwhelming emotions of sadness, and at times the sheer weight of the stories they heard. They saw emotions not as problems in the process of research but more as a bridge or a way by which the research processes held together. Reflexivity through examining their emotions allowed the researchers to find and locate their position in the research. An attention to their emotions also led them to investigate aspects of the research that might have otherwise been overlooked.

Scholars have examined reflexivity to unpack its layers. According to Ryan (2007) we can engage in different forms of reflexivity.

Introspection may be one type of reflexivity that is based upon an experiential encounter in the field. An experience may provide an emotional opening that allows the researcher to empathize with a situation, a belief system, or a practice in the lives of research participants. This may in turn lead to an insight about a group, activity, or culture. The following sections provide various approaches to reflexivity.

Systematic reflexivity (Ryan, 2007) would be an inquiry into one's pre-existing assumptions regarding theory and methods of investigation, while **epistemic reflexivity** would be an examination of one's beliefs and assumptions. These beliefs and assumptions would include examining the research questions to uncover the extent to which the question limited the findings of the research. It would also mean a deliberate awareness of how the research design or analytical process shaped the findings or results of the research. Brockbank and McGill (1998) cautioned that self-reflection could result in researchers strengthening their own beliefs rather than critically deconstructing or analyzing them. Critical approaches to reflexivity can counter this possibility by turning a critical gaze upon oneself with a view to aligning oneself with the purpose of emancipation, a core component of critical research.

Critical Reflexivity

Brookfield (1985) and Fook (2002) explained that critical reflective practice or critical reflection involves thinking about one's actions and systematically analyzing the assumptions and the processes by which the skills or habits of thought have been nurtured. While they use the term "reflective" rather than "reflexivity," their description aligns with our use of the latter term. The first step in critical reflection therefore means learning to understand experiences in a social context and to link knowledge to actions in the present and to future theories of practice.

Bronwyn et al. (2004) considered another dimension of reflexivity by examining the power of discourse and language to consider how language constitutes and contributes to the ways in which the world is constructed. By being more aware of reflexivity in language, a critical approach would examine the language and discourse of equity, inclusion, and exclusion so that the rhetoric and the actions are in tune with each other.

The importance of reflexivity is rarely contested by qualitative inquiry scholars; however, it is true that the discussions around reflexive methods, the specific challenges that researchers can encounter, as well as how reflexivity-as-praxis operates are less often discussed. Examining one's positionality is part of the reflexive process. Positionality involves being transparent about one's identities: class, race, gender, ideas are all subject to self-scrutiny. To be explicit about one's positionality in research projects can also help towards an understanding of a theory of knowledge that is then explained in the research project. Positionality for qualitative researchers is identity work. And these practices can often be guided by intersectionality theories of identity (Christensen and Jensen, 2012; Crenshaw, 1991; Hankivsky et al., 2012).

According to Marcus (1995, p. 111), reflexivity is about "redesigning the observed" and "redesigning the observer." Redesigning the observed means acknowledging that participants are diverse and cannot be subsumed under any one category. Similarly, redesigning the observer means exercising reflexivity so that different ideas, pathways and possibilities open up regarding what is being studied or observed.

Mruck and Breuer (2003), in the excerpt below, remind us of how influential the predominant scientific conventions can still be when we enter qualitative inquiry projects and how these conditions are the very thing we are working against when we actively engage in critical reflexivity processes:

> Although many qualitative researchers now acknowledge that scientific results are dependent on the specific conditions of location and time and contingent on the specific persons involved, the (inter-) subjective modes of constructing knowledge are hardly ever discussed publicly as the *outcome of research*. Even in many empirical studies, by explicitly taking constructionist perspectives, the researcher—inter-acting, choosing, pre-supposing, sympathetic—becomes invisible in favor of mirroring "the other," the object, the phenomenon. Once again, research results resemble photographs that apparently need neither camera nor photographer to exist.
>
> (Mruck and Breuer, 2003, paragraph 9)

Developing various ways to engage in critical reflexivity is an important dimension of the work of qualitative researchers and ought to be as thoughtfully planned out as any other dimension of the methodological moves made in a qualitative inquiry project. Reflexivity processes all require deep questioning of one's assumptions, beliefs, insights, attitudes, interests, curiosities, etc. as they play out within the interpretive dimensions of any study. The questions or prompts that researchers use to examine these various aspects of their meaning-making ought to help them stretch beyond their comfortable interpretations and understandings and place them in an active state of creating new knowledge about the topic of their study in relation to their own positionality (circumstances created in part by the social world in which they inhabit and the human constructs of meaning generally associated with categories). Critical reflexivity processes require the researcher to be acutely aware of, and interact with, the social locations that shape perceptions of the world, the self, and all elements of the study. The more explicit and transparent the audit trail for reflexivity processes can be, the better. And as crucial as these processes are to the overall meaning-making we do as qualitative researchers, it is perhaps the most difficult part to translate into writing without falling into a series of writing traps where the representation of this intellectual work is either underdone or overdone, or written too obtrusively or opaquely, or spread too thinly throughout the entire manuscript, or lumped all together in one section.

Using certain types of questions to guide the critical reflexivity process, and then other questions to help guide the writing and placement of that writing in the manuscript, are activities that are continuously threaded throughout the research project. Here are some examples that will help prepare the ground for the critical reflexivity that we as qualitative researchers need to explicate for our projects. The documentary research of Richard Chalfen (1981), in which he distinguished between two sets of participants who record movies of their choice, is an example of how one can consider reflexivity. One group takes movies about themselves (like the selfies of today) and the other group takes movies external to themselves (like photographs of what we like or see). Chalfen distinguishes the two groups by naming them "look at me" versus "look at me see." For reflexivity, we are often thinking of a combination of the two. While we are recording what we see, we are also saying "look at me in the process of what I see so that you see what I see and understand why I see it the way I do." Some researchers believe that too much focus on methodological awareness could result in hindering the progress of the research project. For example, Seale (1999) contends that there needs to be a balance between methodological awareness and the actual conducting of a research project. Methodological awareness needs to be part of the research project so that awareness serves to strengthen the project and provide deeper resonances.

Tools for Critical Reflexivity Using Questions

Learning from what has worked for other qualitative researchers is always instructive and we have provided in this section a few powerful examples in order to help with the process of building study-specific critical reflexivity plans.

1. Self-Interviewing Questions

There are many forms of self-interviewing that have positive benefits.

The following publications discuss the role self-interviewing played as part of the reflexivity plan employed. In the case of Bolam, Gleeson and Murphy (2003) they had a member of their research team ask the first author the same questions they used within their participant interviews using the protocol they developed. Then they coded and analyzed that data to further inform their own data-analysis process. Other forms of self-interviewing may not use the data alongside other collected data, but rather use it in a research journal for continued examination and discernment as the data-analysis process progresses. And yet another example of a self-interviewing strategy is when it is employed at the start of a project to help refine an interview protocol—not replacing a peer-debriefing strategy for refining a protocol, but adding another layer of interrogation to the process.

2. Critical Reflection Questions

Critical reflexivity involves various forms of critical reflection. Reflection is a term often found in the qualitative research methodological literature, and at times seems to be conflated with the term reflexivity; yet for our purposes we hold these terms as companion terms with distinctions, whereby reflection is a subset or part of the larger, more broadly encompassing activities that fall under the term reflexivity.

Brookfield (1988) developed a four-staged process for critical reflection for educators thinking about pedagogy, yet this process can be easily adapted for the purpose of critical reflexivity for qualitative researchers as they push their thinking toward the intentional development of different perspectives. See, for example, how Kuehne (2016) summarized Brookfield's stages as he adapted them for his study on interviewing farmers and his methodological notes about reflection (*italics* added):

> *assumption analysis*, which is about developing a self-awareness of the assumptions underlying beliefs, values, behaviors, and social structures and then assessing them against lived experience; *contextual awareness*, which is a realization that the above assumptions exist in a historical and cultural context; *imaginative speculation*, which involves seeking out different ways of thinking about the subject of reflection to challenge existing knowledge; *reflective skepticism*, which is a process of questioning claims of truth using the combination of: assumption analysis; contextual awareness, and imaginative speculation.
>
> (Kuehne, 2016, paragraph 43)

Try It Out: Research Journal Exercise 4.1

Using Brookfield's categories, use Table 4.1 to try sketching out a series of questions related to one of your qualitative inquiry projects and then develop a response for each question. Next invite a critical friend to ask you another set of questions and, finally, write responses to the questions posed by your critical friend.

TABLE 4.1 Mapping Questions

Types of Critical Reflection Questions	Your Questions	Your Responses	Your Critical Friend's Questions	Your Responses to Your Critical Friend's Questions
Assumption Analysis				
Contextual Awareness				
Imaginative Speculation				
Reflective Skepticism				

After completing the writing exercise prompted by Table 4.1, the next step would be to convert this writing into action steps within the manuscript. What portions might be added to help create methodological transparency? What portions might help redirect or further guide the methodological moves you will make next in terms of data collection or data analysis?

The critical questioning process helps unfold all dimensions of the qualitative research project.

3. Questions Surrounding the Art of Hearing and Seeing Data

Another example of ways to develop questions concerning the various ways we interact with data is the recognition that questions are shaped by what we hear and see. The following ways are all ripe for being interpreted as sites for more and different kinds of questions that help guide a project: listening to recorded interviews; looking at artifacts, documents, and materials; sketching anything from places where interviews were conducted; and using forms of sketchnotes to help think through a qualitative project.

The following questions can serve as a starting point for questioning data reflexively and paying closer attention to how our positionality may influence how we see and hear:

1. What am I hearing?
2. What am I not hearing? (emphasis on "I")
3. What am I listening to and what am I interpreting?
4. What am I seeing?
5. What am I not seeing?
6. How am I interpreting what I see?
7. What would this look like to another person? (For example, what would a room look like to a teacher versus a student?)

These speculative questions can stimulate further questions regarding reflexivity and data.

Questions during the Writing Up of the Research Report

The end product of a study, referred to generically as the research report, may be in the form of a dissertation or a refereed journal article, a conference presentation, or a public exhibit or performance. All varieties of research reports contain a compressed snapshot, or the essential pieces/essence of what was important in the research. During the writing-up process, we find that questions serve as a reminder of what is important to record in the final report and what contributed to the write-up. It is important to note, and reflect on, the reality that there will always be a process of selection and deselection; various parts of the research data will be included and others excluded. Sets of fieldnotes, full transcripts, reflective memos/logs, or other forms of data are not meant to all make it into the final research report. Therefore, what questions might help guide the selection process?

The starting questions are:

1. Who are the primary and secondary audiences for the report?
2. What are the writing, presentation, exhibit, or performance guidelines that must be adhered to?

3. What story do I want to tell?
4. Whose story is this?
5. What insights do I want to present?
6. How do I present these insights?
7. What is the voice I want to use?
8. Am I distanced from or close to the participants and to the events as I relate them?

Researchers need to wrestle with the imagined or presumed audience(s) in order to determine the "voice" or narration to be used in the writing as well as the guideline expectations that need to be used to build the container that will hold the report.

Summary and Closing Thoughts

Isador I. Rabi, the Nobel Laureate in Physics, credited his mother for "making him a scientist without ever intending it." During an interview he explained what he meant. While every other mother would ask her child after school, "So did you learn anything today?," Isador Rabi said, "Not my mother. She always asked me a different question. 'Izzy,' she would say, 'did you ask a good question today?' That difference—asking good questions—made me become a scientist" (Sheff, 1988). Einstein is reported to have said that if he had an hour to solve a problem and his life depended on it, he would use the first fifty-five minutes to determine the right question to ask and use the remaining five minutes to solve it. When feminist scholars started to ask critical questions that arose out of concerns of women as members of communities, they challenged prevailing assumptions. By asking "where were the women and what were they doing?" (Boxer, 2001, p. 17), feminist scholars opened lines of inquiry into several disciplines that spawned a knowledge revolution and created the basis for women's studies.

In closing, we draw from Susanne Langer's (1942/2009) thoughts on questions as well as John Dewey (1910). Both Dewey and Langer point to the importance of remaining in a state of uncertainty and to pursue inquiry even while doubting or questioning. A caution from Langer (1942/2009) reminds us that, "the way a question is asked limits and disposes the ways in which any answer to it—right or wrong—may be given" (p. 3). Her words point to the central issue we have raised in this book about critical approaches to questions in qualitative research. Our intent in this book was to use questions as a tool and as a strategy—to stimulate deeper thinking and awareness, fuel curiosity while nurturing doubt and uncertainty, and find alternatives to predispositions and settled ways of thinking. The questions and suggestions in this book, we hope, continue to create openings for the art and craft of questioning for qualitative researchers.

References

Bolam, B., Gleeson, K., & Murphy, S. (2003). "Lay Person" or "Health Expert"? Exploring theoretical and practical aspects of reflexivity in qualitative health research [34 paragraphs]. *Forum Qualitative Sozialforschung/ Forum: Qualitative Social Research, 4*(2), Art. 26. Retrieved from http:// nbn-resolving.de/urn:nbn:de:0114-fqs0302266.

Boxer, M.J. (2001). *When women ask the questions: Creating women's studies in America.* Baldimore, MD: Johns Hopkins University Press.

Brockbank, A., & McGill, I. (1998). *Facilitating reflective learning in higher education.* Buckingham: SRHE and Open University Press.

Bronwyn, D., Browne, J., Gannon, S., Honan, E., Laws, C., Mueller-Rockstroh, B., et al. (2004). The ambivalent practices of reflexivity. *Qualitative Inquiry, 10,* 360–389.

Brookfield, S. (1985). *Self-directed learning: From theory to practice* (No. 25). San Francisco, CA: Jossey-Bass.

Brookfield, S. (1988). Developing critically reflective practitioners: A rationale for training educators of adults. In Brookfield, S. (Ed.), *Training educators of adults: The theory and practice of graduate adult education* (pp. 317–38). London: Routledge.

Chalfen, R. (1981). Redundant imagery: Some observations on the use of snapshots in American culture. *Journal of American Culture, 4*(1), 106–113.

Christensen, A.D., & Jensen, S.Q. (2012). Doing intersectional analysis: Methodological implications for qualitative research. *NORA-Nordic Journal of Feminist and Gender Research, 20*(2), 109–125.

Crenshaw, K. (1991). Mapping the margins: Intersectionality, identity politics, and violence against women of color. *Stanford Law Review, 43*(6), 1241–1299.

Dewey, J. (1910). *How we think.* Boston, MA: DC Heath.

Fook, J. (2002). *Social work: Critical theory and practice.* London: Sage.

Hankivsky, O., Grace, D., Hunting, G., Ferlatte, O., Clark, N., Fridkin, A., & Lavoilette, T. (2012). Intersectionality-based policy analysis. In O. Hankivsky (Ed.), *An intersectionality-based policy analysis framework* (pp. 33–45).Vancouver: Institute for Intersectionality Research and Policy, Simon Fraser University.

Hesse-Biber, S.N., & Leavy, P. (2007). *Feminist research practice: A primer.* Thousand Oaks, CA: Sage.

Kuehne, Geoff. (2016). Eight issues to think about before interviewing farmers [62 paragraphs]. *Forum Qualitative Sozialforschung/Forum: Qualitative Social Research, 17*(2), Art. 20. Retrieved from http://nbn-resolving.de/urn:nbn:de:0114-fqs1602205.

Langer, S.K. (1942/2009). *Philosophy in a new key: A study in the symbolism of reason, rite, and art.* Cambridge, MA: Harvard University Press.

Leary, D., Minichiello,V., & Kottler, J.A. (2009). Radical reflexivity in qualitative research. In V. Minichiello & J.A. Kottler (Eds.), *Qualitative journeys: Student and mentor experiences with research* (pp. 49–69).Thousand Oaks, CA: Sage.

Lincoln,Y.S., & Guba, E.G. (2003). Paradigmatic controversies, contradictions, and emerging confluences. In N.K. Denzin &Y.S. Lincoln (Eds.), *The landscape of qualitative research* (2nd ed., pp. 253–291).Thousand Oaks, CA: Sage.

Marcus, G. (1995).The redesign of ethnography after the critique of its rhetoric. In R. Goodman & W. Fisher (Eds.), *Rethinking knowledge: Reflections across the disciplines* (pp. 103–121).Albany: SUNY Press.

Mruck, Katja, & Breuer, Franz. (2003). Subjectivity and reflexivity in qualitative research—the FQS issues [17 paragraphs]. *Forum Qualitative Sozialforschung/Forum: Qualitative Social Research, 4*(2), Art. 23. Retrieved from http://nbn-resolving.de/urn:nbn:de:0114-fqs0302233.

Ryan, T.G. (2007). Leading while looking back and within: Reflective and reflexive modes. In Saran Donahoo & Richard C. Hunter (Eds.), *Teaching leaders to lead teachers,* Advances in educational administration,Vol. 10. (pp. 365–372). Bingley: Emerald Group Publishing Limited.

Seale, C. (1999). *The quality of qualitative research.* London: Sage.

Sheff, D. (1988, January 12). Letter to the editor. *New York Times.* Retrieved July 23, 2016, from http://www.nytimes.com/1988/01/19/opinion/l-izzy-did-you-ask-a-good-question-today-712388.html.

Sparkes,A. (2002). *Telling tales in sport and physical activity: A qualitative journey.* Champaign, IL: Human Kinetics Publishers.

Taylor, C. (1995).The dialogical self. In R.F. Goodman & W.R. Fisher (Eds.), *Rethinking knowledge: Reflections across the disciplines* (pp. 57–66). NewYork, NY: SUNY Press.

Van Maanen, J. (2011). *Tales of the field: On writing ethnography.* Chicago, IL: University of Chicago Press.

INDEX